Take a Stand

A Story of Tenacity,
Courage, Brotherhood,
and Commitment

To:

Ed. -

" Think Deep "

Best -

[signature]

12-09-11

Take a Stand

A Story of Tenacity,
Courage, Brotherhood,
and Commitment

Mike Cattolico
LCDR, USN (Retired)

Grassroots Publishing Group
Carlsbad, California
www.GrassrootsPublishingGroup.com

Grassroots Publishing Group™
1824 Oak Ave
Carlsbad, CA 92008
www.GrassrootsPublishingGroup.com

10 9 8 7 6 5 4 3 2
First Edition Published 2011
Printed in the United States of America

ISBN-10: 0-9794805-2-3
ISBN-13: 978-0-9794805-2-2
Library of Congress Control Number: 2011922573

Cover artwork by Rick Armstrong
Cover & book design by CenterPointe Media
www.CenterPointeMedia.com

Mixed Sources
Product group from well-managed
forests and other controlled sources
www.fsc.org Cert no. SW-COC-002283
© 1996 Forest Stewardship Council
FSC

ACKNOWLEDGEMENTS

Writing a book is not an easy task, especially for a sailor. Salty language is hard to contain, but my wife gently and persistently pushed me to clean up my act. I offer her a special thank you for her encouragement and patience. I did the best I could not to embarrass anyone. Some expressions just slipped through the cracks. Sorry!

My mother always encouraged me to get an education. She said that an education was a "chest of tools." She was right—mothers are always right. I am grateful to her for her advice. My dad told me to get a good government job, and I am thankful to him, as well. In the end I listened to both of them—I went to lots of school and served in the U. S. Navy. I hope that I satisfied my parents in my many endeavors, and I hope that they are now sitting on a puffy, white cloud giving me a thumbs-up. In many ways, this story is a tribute to them.

I would like to acknowledge Nesta Aharoni of Grassroots Publishing Group for her editorial and publishing expertise. I also would like to acknowledge Matthew and Joan Greenblatt of CenterPointe Media for their talent and creativity.

Readers, thank you for taking the time to examine my thoughts and my life. It is my sincere hope that I have entertained and enlightened you.
—Mike Cattolico

CONTENTS

PREFACE

I often joked with my parents about why World War II ended when it did: because somehow the Axis powers found out that I was coming into the world in September 1945! I have always expected a lot of myself, and I have led an unusual, diverse, and productive life. After many acquaintances exclaimed, "Man, you ought to write a book about all the things you've done!" I took pen to paper (literally) and began to recount memories as they unfolded.

Many authors imply that their work could turn them into overnight successes, improve their personal status, or dramatically change their lives. My intention is humbler than that. I am a storyteller who likes to share insights into the baby boomer generation. I am an educator and coach who eagerly shares character-building lessons. I am a navy diver who enjoys delivering messages about service and devotion.

This book contains stories that are comical, heartbreaking, intriguing, and for some, controversial. It is a compilation of vignettes … stories of a man's life, a U.S. Navy diver's life. You will encounter tales of accomplishments that were achieved under the most adverse conditions and accounts of a life's failures. Readers may wonder why anyone would voluntarily subject himself to such highs and lows … but therein lies the tale.

Although baby boomers will find this content richly familiar, it was not written just for them. It also was written for subsequent generations who neither faced our obstacles nor enjoyed our benefits. Later generations may discover truths they can apply to their own times, just as the baby boomers discovered truths from those who lived through the Great Depression and the Second World War.

Take a Stand is a book about helping people and being personally rewarded for the effort. The lessons presented touch on responsibility, courage, and self-discovery, and on what constitutes a successful life … apart from great riches, political power, or greed. Also included are extraordinary insights into the value of friendship, loyalty, and yes, patriotism.

Mine has been a life of service—a life well lived. Read on and enjoy. Together we can make America a better place.

—Mike Cattolico

CHAPTER ONE

INSTILLING VALUES AND BUILDING COURAGE

"There is no greater agony than bearing
an untold story inside you."
–Maya Angelou

One of my favorite movies is *Tombstone* with Wyatt Earp, Doc Holliday, and lots of thrilling cowboy stuff. Many movies were made about Wyatt Earp and the O. K. Corral, some legend and some factual. I have seen most of them—all worth watching—but some are better than others. I liked *Tombstone* best because of its ending. When Doc Holliday was on his deathbed with tuberculosis, Wyatt visits him in the sanatorium. Holliday asks Earp, "What do you want, Wyatt?" Earp answers, "Just a normal life, Doc." Doc counters, "There's no normal life, Wyatt … just life."

Life imparts many lessons. These lessons can build integrity and cultivate values. For me, character building started when I was very young and continued throughout my life.

I was two when my father started taking me to Sylvi's Bar and Grill on Pike Street, Philadelphia, to dance on the bar. My dad was Italian, and that's where all of the Italian guys hung out. I didn't realize then what a celebrity I was, but I suppose it had something to do with my light skin, milk-white hair, and thirst for attention.

My mother, a Scotch-English redhead, was originally a farm girl from a coal mining town in Western Pennsylvania. Although she was a newcomer to the Italian clan, she was immediately accepted into the community. She was a registered nurse who helped many immigrant people during and after the difficult World War II times.

Because my dad was a machinist at the Philadelphia Naval Shipyard, he was given a Presidential pardon by Roosevelt to be draft exempt during WWII. He fervently loved America, and he never seemed to get over not having served in uniform. He and I rarely entertained that sensitive subject, even after I grew older.

After the war, Mother (which was how I always addressed her) tolerated city life for a while, but around 1950 she gave my dad an ultimatum—"I will no longer tolerate this concrete jungle, the Italian mindset, and your family telling me what to do. We either move to a farm, or I'm history." Although Mother was a compassionate person, she was willful and decisive. No one wanted to get on her bad side ... ever.

For $4,500 my parents purchased a small, five-acre farm about thirty miles outside the city. That amount of money was considered big bucks in 1950. The property had a ramshackle house and a broken-down garage that only stayed upright because it was buttressed by a rusted-out 1936 Ford.

The house was only a shell: no heat, no water, no toilet—no nothing. We survived with piles of blankets until Dad installed a coal heater and some old radiators. With the help of my dad's best friend, plumber Tom Davis, we dug a well, installed a pump, and connected everything. Voila! We had heat. What a luxury. The toilet (no silent lid), bathtub, and sink were the next to arrive. We were on a roll. We hand dug a cesspool (septic), filled it with rocks, started the interior wall plastering (drywall had not yet been invented), installed a cook stove and used Hotpoint refrigerator, and at last, began living like human beings. Not surprisingly, we were assigned water hours and allowed to bathe once a week. Dad was paranoid about the well going dry and the cesspool filling.

Both of my parents were products of the Great Depression. Nothing—I mean *nothing*—was wasted or thrown away. Because Dad was a gifted mechanic, he could fabricate, change, build, or demolish anything with his two hands. I learned a great deal from him. Yet as I viewed it at that time, he had one fault: He lacked a sense of security. He could be a risk taker to a degree, but not all out. A guaranteed weekly paycheck was his security. Back then I had a problem with that, but years later I grew to understand why. Supporting his family was his motivation. I learned to respect him for his patience, love, concern, endurance, and tenacity.

My father's depression-era traits were demonstrated the day my mother decided to take up basic farming. We didn't have a barn, but that didn't stop her from keeping animals—chickens, ducks, sheep, calves, and more—in the cellar. The accumulation of animal waste got to be unbearable, so the next order of business was, "Tony, we need a barn." I was six years old at that time. Dad and I picked a spot and hand dug the barn's footings until they were below the frost line, three feet deep and two feet wide. Next we erected batter boards, hand mixed the concrete, and started laying cinder block walls. Try to imagine a six-year-old today carrying one cinder block in each hand and mixing concrete with a hoe. Nowadays that would probably be considered prosecutable child abuse. The principle imposed by my parents was "you don't work, you don't eat." Since I have always had a pathological fondness for eating, that rule was clear enough to me.

My dad used what psychologists today might call a cross between positive and negative reinforcement. For example; after I asked, "Hey, Dad, where are we going to get the wood for the roof?" his response was, "Follow me, Son." Soon we were tearing down a fifty-year-old barn that a neighbor wanted demolished, loading the lumber onto a wagon towed by a 1938 Chevy, and hauling the load to our new barn. We cut that lumber by hand (no power saws in those days) to craft trusses and planks. Believe me when I tell you that hand-sawing a fifty-year-old beam is brutal work.

Into the barn came the sheep, cows, chickens, ducks and pigs, and all of them had to be fed. Work was abundant. Here is a list of my summer activities: plant corn, beans, and vegetables; cut and rake hay (hand rakes, no tractor); stow the hay in the top floor of the barn (in Pennsylvania summer heat); clean the manure out of the pens; broadcast the manure on the hay fields; harvest the corn; pick and weed strawberries and beans; and hand-ax oak trees to increase hayfield areas. Winter activities: plow or, rather, shovel snow; hand-ax more trees; build more barn pens and chicken houses; feed the animals; and of course, attend school.

My year-round activities consisted of hand carrying twenty-four buckets of water from the house to the barn animals—twenty-four buckets in the morning and twenty-four at night. In the summer the water carrying wasn't too bad, but in the winter, it bordered on torture. I was only four feet eleven inches when I was a high school sophomore, and that was after a growth spurt. The distance between the house and the barn measured 520 feet. Winter required hot water to melt the ice in the barn pens, and that meant carrying twenty-four buckets of water 520 feet while holding the containers shoulder high above the snow drifts. Twelve trips up and twelve back. Who needed a gym to get into shape?

My summers were not all work and no play. Don't underestimate the energy and inventiveness of the American child. Twice weekly Mother would take me to the Chalfont Swimming Pool for two hours. This was heaven. In addition, I managed to sneak in some leisure activity between my work responsibilities. I fashioned bows and arrows from tree saplings and chicken feathers, ran trap lines, caught and skinned muskrat and skunk, and sold pelts for twenty cents each. I fished in the local lake and slept in the hay mow. My closest friend lived three miles away, and we walked and biked to see each other. He and I discovered that if we blew up balloons and tied them to the forks of our bikes, they sounded like hot rod motors when they hit the spokes.

My daily school-year schedule was something like this:

Monday through Friday

    5:30 A.M.

        Rise and shine

        Feed and water the animals

        Prepare for school

    8:00 A.M.

Arrive at school

Note: St Joseph Catholic grade school had only one bus, a 1951 Chevy that was driven by Mr. Ford, whose alcoholic breath could wrinkle a freshly starched shirt ... morning and afternoon.

3:30 P.M.

Arrive home and feed and water the animals

Start homework

Eat dinner

Finish homework

Wash and dry the dishes

After chores and homework

Bed (no TV, games, or other entertainment)

Saturday

7:00 A.M.

Rise and shine

Meet the milkman for the weekly purchase of a half gallon of ice cream

Throughout the day

Work the farm

After work

Bed

Sunday

5:45 A.M.

Rise and shine

6:30 A.M.

Mass at St. Joseph Church (earliest mass so that we had extra time to work)

4:00 P.M.

Homework

After homework

Bed

This rigorous schedule continued for years with one alteration, which was made in 1953. Until that time the only downtime we had was sleep.

The one alternation was a big one—a television set. It arrived in the form of a monstrous Zenith box with a round screen that played three channels: channels 3, 6, and 10. The biggest surprise was a guy named Howdy Doody who offered a half hour of uninterrupted ecstasy. I watched Howdy Doody, Buffalo Bob, Indian Princess puppet, Mr. Bluster, Dilly Dally, and Clarabell the clown. I related to the puppets and Buffalo Bob but had reservations about the big guy dressed as a clown who squirted water at everyone with his seltzer bottle. But it was all good, wholesome fun.

Fear and courage come in different forms at different ages. The Early Show came on the TV at 5 P.M., so I hurriedly performed my daily duties so I could catch a movie. They were broadcasting *The Thing,* an early horror show about the discovery of a frozen monster who wreaks havoc as he defrosts. The Thing was played by six-foot six-inch James Arness, of later *Gunsmoke* fame. To make Arness appear even taller, the costumers put him in platform shoes. The Thing was awesome in its size and strength and terrifying in its actions. Biblically speaking, as a lad of eight I was "sore afraid."

One of my nightly jobs was to close and lock the chicken house door so that the foxes and weasels could not devastate the hen house. Each night my dad asked this inevitable question: "Did you lock the chicken house?" Oh, merciful God, how was I ever going to survive those 520 feet to the barn knowing full well that the scientists may not have really killed The Thing and that it was out there in the dark waiting for me?

People say that courage is the ability to act even when you are scared half to death. Further, they say that if you look at fear firmly in the face and overcome it, you will be a better person. At that youthful time in my life, I thought I was already a pretty good person and didn't need to be any better. But courage prevailed—kind of. I never could have admitted to anyone that I was scared—especially to my dad. So off I ran to the chicken house. Every crunch of snow and every tree that was distorted into The Thing fueled the adrenalin that propelled my little feet.

CHAPTER TWO
BE TRUE TO YOURSELF

"If Benjamin Franklin had tried to be general and George
Washington had tried to be an inventor, we would probably
still be living in a British Colony without electricity."
–Unknown

MEMORIES

After I more or less overcame my basic fear of *The Thing*, new programs emerged on the "boob tube." Soon we were flooded with half-hour shows and series that highlighted good guys. Here's a short list for baby boomers to reminisce about:

The Lone Ranger	The Bounty Hunter	Wanted: Dead or
Roy Rogers	The Rifleman	Alive
Gene Autry	Bonanza	Zorro
Hopalong Cassidy	Broken Arrow	The Cisco Kid
Have Gun-Will	Lawman	The Range Rider
Travel	Maverick	Sky King
Gunsmoke	Cheyenne	Rawhide
Colt 45	Sugarfoot	

These cowboy heroes never failed. Within a thirty-minute span of time, they located the bad guy, saved the West from every imaginable evil, and rode victoriously into the sunset. Well, most of the time, anyway. Television programming expanded from predominantly offering westerns to offering a variety of other types of shows.

The Flying Nun	Baretta
Davy Crockett	Ironside
77 Sunset Strip	Alfred Hitchcock
Route 66	Presents
Mission: Impossible	Sea Hunt

These TV shows were weaved into the lifestyles of kids who survived the 1940s, '50s, and '60s. But there were many more things we had in common.

- The mothers who delivered us smoked and/or drank while they were pregnant … and we survived. They took aspirin, ate blue cheese dressing, consumed tuna from a can, and never got tested for diabetes.
- At naptime and nighttime we were placed on our tummies in cribs that were coated with brightly colored, lead-based paints. Medicine bottles had no childproof lids; doors and cabinets had no locks; and when we rode our bikes, we wore no helmets. One common source of transportation—we hitchhiked.
- When we were infants and young children, we rode in cars without car seats, booster seats, seat belts, or air bags. Riding in the back of a pickup truck on a warm day was a special treat.
- We drank water from a garden hose—*not* from a designer bottle. Four friends shared one bottled soft drink—and *no one* died.
- We ate cupcakes, white bread, and real butter. We drank Kool-Aid made with sugar, but we were not overweight because *we were always outside playing or working.*

- Our families were unable to reach us all day, but we were okay. We spent hours building go-carts out of scraps and then screaming down the biggest hill we could find, only to discover that we had neglected to install a critical go-cart component—the brakes. After concluding the ride, not by braking but by a natural application of physical law (shrubs, tree branches, and ditches), we taught ourselves how to solve the deceleration problem.

- We had no PlayStations, Nintendos, or Xboxes. We did not have cable TV with 220 channels, video movies, DVDs, surround sound, CDs, cell phones, personal computers, the Internet, or chat rooms. Instead, *we had friends,* and we went *outdoors* to find them. We fell out of trees. We got cuts, scrapes, broken bones, and chipped teeth, yet there were no lawsuits filed as a result of our behavior. We ate worms and mud pies. The worms did not survive in our bodies forever, and our digestive systems efficiently overpowered whatever creatures lived in that dirt.

- We were given BB guns and .22 caliber rifles for our tenth birthdays. We invented games with sticks and tennis balls, and we did not require the participation of adults to referee or coach them.

- While our mothers warned us about the dangers of certain activities, our fathers declared, "Just let them be kids." According to our mothers, there were only two injuries an active child could sustain, and we were incessantly warned against them. However, despite our mothers' dire predictions, we never broke our back or put someone's eye out.

- When we wanted to visit a friend's house, we rode our bikes or walked. Then we knocked on the door, rang the doorbell, or walked right in to talk to them.

- When youth sports became organized, we went to Little League tryouts. Some of us did not make the team. Those who didn't had to learn to cope with disappointment. Imagine that!

- If we broke the law, our parents did not bail us out. They took a side—the side of the law

The past fifty years have produced an explosion of innovative ideas. The children who were raised in the 1940s, '50s, and '60s have turned out to be some of the most effective risk takers, problem solvers, and inventors ever produced. They are a testament to a philosophy of freedom, failure, success, and responsibility ... and learning to cope with it all.

Are you one of the lucky ones who were raised during the baby boomer time frame? If you are, congratulations! Share this chapter with others who were fortunate enough to grow up before the lawyers and the government regulated so much of our lives for "our own good." While you are at it, forward this chapter to your kids so they will understand how brave (and lucky) their parents were. Kind of makes you want to run through the house with scissors, doesn't it?

Baby boomers, count the items from the list below that you remember, not the ones you were merely told about.

1. Black Jack chewing gum
2. Wax Coca-Cola-shaped bottles filled with colored sugar water
3. Candy cigarettes
4. Soda pop machines that dispensed glass soda bottles
5. Coffee shops or diners with tableside jukeboxes
6. Milk delivered to your door in glass bottles with cardboard stoppers
7. Telephone party lines
8. Newsreels and cartoons shown in movie theaters before the movie
9. P F Flyers
10. Butch wax
11. TV test patterns that came on at night after the last show and then blankness on the screen until programming started again in the morning. (There were only three available channels.)
12. Peashooters
13. Howdy Doody
14. 78 rpm records
15. S&H Green Stamps
16. Hi-fis
17. Metal ice trays with levers
18. Mimeograph paper
19. Blue flashbulbs
20. Packard automobiles
21. Roller skate keys
22. Cork popguns
23. Drive-in theaters
24. Studebakers
25. Washtub wringers

We had hideouts in long-forgotten, candlelit potato cellars, and we didn't suffocate. For fifty cents an hour we worked a couple of hours on Sundays as trap boys at the local skeet club. This helped us supplement our skunk and muskrat pelt income, which was needed to feed the five cent pinball machines in the bowling alley five miles down the road. Astonishingly, playing the pinball machines did not turn us into degenerate gamblers.

Then in the summer of 1957, out of the clear blue sky, my dad said, "Son, I've decided to run water and electricity to the barn." I couldn't believe my ears. By this time I was a man of the world and knew all about that new invention called a backhoe, a tractor with a big toothed bucket that God, in his infinite wisdom, had created to make life easier for mankind—especially twelve-year-old young men. Occasionally I watched farmers and construction workers use a backhoe to move dirt and rocks with amazing speed and minimal physical effort. They just sat in the seat, worked the levers, and instantly created holes and trenches. Being an innovative and savvy farm boy, I said, "Great, Dad. When do we get the backhoe?" His response? "Come with me, Boy."

Dad handed me a pick and shovel and a quick set of instructions regarding the trench dimensions: "Three feet deep, wide enough to stand in. And you *will* complete it on your summer vacation. You have a choice of fifty cents a day or nothing. What'll it be?"

I quickly assessed the situation. The negative side: This is over and above the "normal" everyday stuff I have to do. This land is riddled with rock and shale, which I learned well when I was digging the barn's footings. I will not have much time for fun things. If I refuse, I lose a pathetic fifty cents a day and gain the wrath of my mother and father. "No" is not an option.

The positive side: I will get long-term relief from carrying water. I will receive payment in full at the end of the project—about thirty bucks. I quickly calculated that I could work June and July to complete the Big Dig and use August to recover at the swimming pool . . . before the dreaded school year began.

My calculations were right on the money. As a matter of fact, I finished the project three days early. My parents were so happy that when the waterlines and cable were placed in the trench and connected, Dad helped me backfill the hole. To express his satisfaction and gratification, he put his hand on my shoulder and said, "Great job!" Who could have asked for more? Then he turned to me and said, "We are going to give thanks to the Blessed Mother Mary by building a small shrine over there. We need water for the waterfall and electricity to light the Madonna statue at night."

Of course, this required another trench, 100 feet long. The Virgin Mary must have had pity on me because this trench wasn't made up of a lot of shale and rocks. Nowadays similar treatment of a child would be considered slavery or child abuse. But that thought didn't occur to anyone in 1957. Instead, my father created in me and then honed a solid work ethic.

SCHOOL

My mother was a proponent of formal education. In fact, she was staunch on the subject. I was not. I was the champion of creating a reason for not excelling in the classroom. She tried the gentle bop-on-the-head trick, the ear-twisting thing, and the positive reinforcement idea (i.e., an extra ration of vanilla fudge ice cream). Nothing worked. I excelled at digging ditches and I proved it. Why can't we leave it at that? Who needs English, civics, geography, history, and arithmetic when, instead, you can have swimming, pinball machines, trapping, and bows and arrows—all performed with enviable skill?

If ever there was support for the theory of Lamarckism (like father like son), I was it. I was mechanical, like Dad. The question always was, "Do you want to be a ditch digger the rest of your life?" Here's what I didn't understand: If my mother thought ditch digging was so dishonorable, why didn't she apply that rationale to my two previous ditches?

My elementary education took place two miles down the road at St. Joseph Parochial School, which was run by the parish priests in the diocese, the pastor (supreme boss), and his curate (second in command). We didn't see too much of the last two, except for at Sunday mass and on special occasions. The nuns (Sacred Heart Order) pretty much ran the show. Apart from a few exceptions, they didn't demonstrate a lot of compassion or tolerance when it came to discipline, pranks, recess, or learning. Their job was to educate, and they used every means imaginable—and unimaginable—to accomplish that mission.

The sixth-grade teacher, Sister Sanctissima, struck absolute fear in the hearts and souls of her students. She had medieval-like torture mechanisms, such as pointers (three-foot long sticks with a very hard rubber tip), yard rulers (flat sticks with metal ends), sideburn and ear twisters (usually her thumb and forefinger), and the infamous "clicker." This devise was diverse and could do many things. It was constructed of wood (oak, I think), conical in shape, had a large rubber band around the middle that connected it to a popsicle-stick-type lever. When the lever was depressed and then released, it made an audible clicking sound. Hence it was known as the "clicker."

We students quickly learned the "clicker" code. For example, one click for stand up; two clicks for sit down; three clicks for genuflect; and so on. It was a very sturdy piece of equipment that, from time to time and depending on the message, also could be used to not so gently "tap" you on your head. All of the nuns had a clicker, but Sister Sanctissima was renowned for more frequent use. I don't believe she was ever happy. The only time I remember seeing her crack a grin during my sixth-grade year was the day the pastor stopped by.

Sanctissima didn't take kindly to anyone, especially me because I squirmed a lot in my desk and I was not good at arithmetic. The reason I squirmed was that my legs were short and hung suspended above the floor when I sat at my desk; this created numbing cramps in my legs throughout the day. Of course, I could never explain that to the sister. To her I was just another kid who wasn't paying attention.

Sister Regina, on the other hand, was a breath of fresh air. Not only was she a classroom teacher, she was also the piano instructor. My mother was ecstatic when I said I wanted to take piano lessons. In her mind that meant there was hope for me. Actually, I didn't want anything to do with the art of music; I just wanted to be around Sister Regina. She was a beautiful, happy, vibrant teacher who personified friendliness, understanding, and compassion, all wrapped up in one penguin outfit. I knew that she knew that I wasn't going to be another Liberace, but she had admirable patience with me.

Last but not least was the mother nun, Mother Majella. In the old Catholic school tradition, when you reached eighth grade, your teacher was the mother nun. Eighth grade was the big time. Mother Majella was old, tired, and wonderful. I suspect that she was in her late sixties or early seventies at that time (which seemed old to an eighth grader). She was not well, and she often experienced nosebleeds that streamed over her white bib. At those times she had to be assisted by other nuns. For the first time in my life I felt sorry for someone and did the best I could to make her proud of me.

Although I was very weak in math, I tried to compensate in other areas. The department I excelled in was recess. I found that I had a unique ability to control the boys in the schoolyard, and they gravitated toward my leadership, which came naturally to me. Often I saw her watching me from the window. Soon I became the safety patrol lieutenant (voted in unanimously by my peers) and was awarded the American Legion medal for leadership. Mother Majella beamed with joy.

One day Mother Majella noticed that I was the last student to leave the classroom at day's end. She approached me as I packed my school bag, which in those days consisted of a surplus WWII ammunition bag (nothing fancy but practical and durable). She put her hands on my shoulders and said, "Michael, don't worry a lot about math. It will come to you someday. Give it time." Then she added words that I have never, ever forgotten: "Someday you will be the leader of men." To this day, whenever I think of her—her kindness, thoughtfulness, compassion, and foresight—that memory triggers more than one tear. Thank you, Mother Majella.

STAMPED IN CONCRETE, CAST IN GRANITE

Before continuing my educational journey, there is one tidbit that I must convey. This essential piece of information filled a gap in my schooling and, ultimately, was the greatest influence in my life. To understand its impact, I must take you back to water—to the swimming pool at Chalfont, Pennsylvania. When I was about eleven, my mother dropped me off at the pool early because she had other things to do and was very confident in my swimming ability and the skill of the lifeguard on duty. Water and I were like peanut butter and jelly, ham and eggs, or steak and potatoes. In short, I was one with water.

As I was checking in to the facility, I noticed a guy standing on the bottom of the pool's deep end, which was ten feet deep. He had some sort of bucket-like object on his head, and air was being pumped to him by a compressor on the surface. He was sweeping the pool from the bottom! This was the most amazing thing I had ever seen—a man breathing underwater! I was captivated and in awe. At that moment, my life changed. I realized that working under water was what I wanted to do with my life. I began to wonder by what magic and by what course of action I could I make this happen. I was infatuated by the mere thought of underwater diving. How soon could I make this happen?

I was not able to answer this question for quite a while. First, I had to reach the end of my long, hard road to a high school diploma. At the time I was introduced to underwater diving I was approaching the end of grade school and the beginning of high school. I impatiently thought that the world would end before I could even attempt anything like it. But the idea of an underwater career prompted me to get my priorities straight. Doing well in high school could be a sign to my parents that I had finally seen the light and found the error of my ways. My high school performance could be the ticket I needed to convince my mom and dad that I was not a hopeless case. Meanwhile, there were many bridges to cross before I could reach that crowning moment.

Bishop McDevitt High School was tough (as were all of the other Catholic schools). The first order of business was to determine how to get to the school and how to return home. The school was sixteen miles from our farmhouse. My only available transportation was a local high school junior who had his driver's license and a '54 Chevy. If Jim didn't go to school one day, none of his riders did either, including me.

Then there was the curriculum—Latin, French, algebra, geometry, English … and discipline. The discipline was the easiest to handle and seemed to have a purpose. The priests must have learned their style of discipline at the hands of the German SS; to them we were the local "farmers" who didn't have time for sports or any other school functions. We were a small group who kept to ourselves, and we were somewhat ostracized for it. Then there were the academics: Who cared that 1A + 1B = 2AB, what the hypotenuse of an angle is, that Caesar fought the Gallic Wars, or how to correctly say "good morning" in French?

My underwater diving plan started to quickly unravel when I came home with four—yes, four—failure notices that acknowledged my academic ineptitude. Each had to be signed by my parents. It was obvious that I had to take another course of action, and fast. A deal, that's it; I'll make a deal with my parents. If I'm permitted to take a basic scuba course at the YMCA, I'll pull up the grades. My strategy worked. This was my first stroke of genius.

In the meantime, new things appeared on the horizon—sweet sixteen; a license to drive; Saturday night cruising in my mother's '51 Ford, which was equipped with Pep Boys "add-a-whitewall" tires and a noisy Glasspack muffler; and … girls.

Even though these novelties were all around, my underwater adventures took center stage in my life, and I did keep up my grades—well, sort of. Then I received another ultimatum from the home front: "If you don't get your head screwed on right, how will you ever get into college?"

Lord, help me! College? All I wanted to do was go underwater. Couldn't anyone see that? After all, I was almost seventeen years old, and I knew exactly what I wanted to do. At this point in the conversation, Mother started to cry. Dad shook his head and called me a dummy—among other things—and I felt like a complete disappointment.

"Okay." I said. "If it's college you want, then it's college you are going to get." But the question was this: How was I going to qualify to get into college? The answer was this: barely. In my first year at Temple University, Philadelphia, they put me on probation. Definitely not a great start. I was not an academician, and no one was going to change that fact. To me college was like trying to paint over rust. You can brush it on, roll it on, or spray it on, but inevitably the rust comes through.

My freshman year was a disaster. The dean gave me one more semester to pull up my grades to a C average GPA. If that feat was not accomplished, I would no longer be a matriculating student at Temple University. My mother felt let down. She was working as a night nurse to pay for my tuition. How could I have let such a thing happen? I felt lower than low. Now was the time to rise up and prove that I was not a total jerk. Miraculously, with nonstop determination and less time scuba diving, I mustered a 2.26 GPA, a little above a C average. For the time being, I was saved.

One night while I was attending a briefing at the university by Jacques Cousteau, co- inventor of the U. S. Diver's aqualung, I bumped into Tom Smith. Tom was wearing a jacket with a large patch on the back that read "Telford Diving Unit, Organized 1947." The Telford Diving Unit was the only volunteer underwater rescue and recovery unit in the United States that utilized the Mark (MK) V, the U.S. Navy deep sea diving apparatus. The Mark V made Mike Nelson on the TV series Sea Hunt look like a sunbather. Had I died and gone to heaven? Jacques Cousteau and navy diving rigs—all in one night! I was at the right place at the right time.

Now was the time to talk over some serious stuff with my parents. "Look, I'm twenty years old and not happy with this college thing. I know that I can excel in the underwater field. It's a direction that can make me very happy. Don't you want to see me happy?" This time I was playing on Mother's emotions—not in order to hurt her but to get her approval and blessing.

She responded, "Go for it and be happy. You have to love what you do. I know you'll succeed." I was at a loss for words. We hugged.

I left Temple University, got a job, enlisted in the navy, and waited. I was happy—very happy. Thank you, Mother.

CHAPTER THREE
DARE TO BEGIN

"All glory comes from daring to begin for
courage mounteth with occasion."
–William Shakespeare

PREPARING TO TAKE OFF

In 1966, while I was waiting for induction into the navy, I landed a job with the Vick Chemical Company, the group that makes Vicks Cough Drops, Nyquil, and other over-the-counter medications. This was a four-month job that paid $2.50 an hour. It carried me through the 120-day navy delay-entry program, and it was an education in its own right.

Because I was a man of innovative spirit, Vick Chemical Company was not exactly my idea of a lifelong vocation, but it did fill a need for a short time. I quickly realized that there were people on this planet who had no other goal in life than to keep conveyor belts packed full with empty bottles. These were "company people" who spent thirty or more years doing the same routine thing every day, week, month, and year. Some of them spent the better part of their adult lives separating broken cough drops from unbroken cough drops.

I am aware that some folks are satisfied with this type of work and happy to have the job. They don't need to think too much; they have no pressing responsibilities; and occasionally they can be promoted to fore-man or another first-line supervisory position. With no denigration to the workers, I understand that some businesses need this type of mindset to fill the jobs that close the circle in the production sector of capitalism. But after working the Lavoris, Formula 44, and Cepacol lines and witnessing a coworker almost drown in a Clearasil vat (which probably prevented pimples in his family line for generations afterward), I was happy to leave, and they were happy to see me go. Maybe that had something to do with my parting comment to them, "Give a monkey a banana, and he could do the same thing."

Meanwhile, I was very involved with the Telford Diving Unit and voted in as a member in good standing. I made an indoctrination dive in the MK V deep sea diving rig. What a rush it was—little Mike clad in fifty-six pounds of helmet and breastplate, eighty-four pounds of lead around the waist, and seventeen and a half pounds for each shoe. The cotton twill vulcanized rubber "dress" was an additional thirty pounds. The complete outfit totaled about 205 pounds. The MK V is a man's rig. It was the official navy rig. I was proving to myself and my fellow divers that I could "cut the mustard" and have plenty to spare. This was the first time in my life that I was not an ordinary somebody. In the MK V, I was somebody special.

We did a lot of quarry diving in Pennsylvania and New Jersey—in big, deep, abandoned holes that were filled with water. One day I spoke with another diver at a quarry in Pennsylvania that acted as a recreational diving spot for scuba divers (it had an old steam shovel at the bottom at fifty feet). As I was speaking with this guy, I noticed a tattoo on his arm. When I looked closer, I saw the navy MK V helmet adorned with dolphins and surrounded by the words "U. S. Navy Deep Sea Diver—We Dive the World Over."

I was enthralled, and we talked even more. He told me that only the best of the best make it into the navy diver program. That was all I needed to hear. I went back to my navy recruiter armed with a new salvo of ques-tions. He assured me that there would be no problem directing me toward a navy diving career. Then I was struck by a tinge of fear. What if I failed?

I began to harbor the prospect of failure. Failure is a repugnant thought. Because of many unknown elements, I was on the verge of obsession, and that was a very dangerous place to be. I was like the ham in ham and eggs: The chicken is involved, but the pig is committed.

Telford Diving Unit

THE SEND-OFF AND BEYOND

The night before I left for basic training (boot camp), the boys at Telford Diving Unit threw a party for me at the local Veterans of Foreign Wars (VFW) post. None of us was a VFW, but the post waived their requirement due to the specialness of the occasion and the fact that the Vietnam conflict was in full swing. A mixture of beverage holders—glasses full of blackberry brandy and mugs full of Black Label beer—made my two-day train trip to Great Lakes, Illinois, a fuzzy but memorable experience.

My first shipmate in the making was Bob Whetstone. After I was able to manifest some semblance of post-drinking coherence, he said he had watched me all night to see if I was going to live. He turned out to be a best friend and, later, a navy corpsman and Vietnam survivor.

Because I was a "natural leader," I was appointed RPOC (Recruit Petty Officer Chief). My job was to keep my company in line when the company commander was absent; in other words, I was the navy equivalent of the much-publicized assistant marine drill instructor.

Military life suited me. It included all of the things I was primed for in my youth: discipline, order, and regimentation. Actually, for me military life was a piece of cake. While everyone else complained, I reveled in it. No ditches to dig, no corn to pick, no animals to feed,

MKV deep sea rig. (Pre-Navy training—Author)

Boot Camp Graduate
Author Leading Company

no water to carry. All I had to do was look smart, do my job, and learn the navy way.

Two weeks before the end of boot camp, the navy interviewer asked me what I wanted to do during my four-year enlistment. My answer to him was, "I want to be a navy deep sea diver." He informed me that in order to achieve that goal, I needed an underwater rating. A "rating" designates a sailor's job. For example, a boatswain's mate works on a ship's deck and maintains all the lines and equipment located there. A yeoman is similar to a secretary. A commissary man is a cook. I needed to have a rating before I could become a specialist, and I could not apply for the specialty until I had advanced in rank to third-class petty officer, the first of the noncommissioned officer ranks, just above seaman.

Bob Whetstone (L) "Corpsman"
and Author

I asked my interviewer what my underwater choices were, and he replied that I should either be a torpedoman or a mineman. I pondered, "If I become a torpedoman and do not make the grade as a diver, I sure as hell am going to find my country ass on a submarine, and I want none of the 'sewer pipe' life. But mineman? Wow!" I was familiar with maritime movies. Mines were big, black balls that were suspended underwater on chains. Mines sank ships. That was for me.

Off I went to Charleston, South Carolina, for mineman training … ten more weeks of school, but necessary to become a diver, so they said.

When I was fresh out of Mineman A school, I was told to take my pick of the mine facility I wanted to be assigned to. My choices were Italy, Iceland, the Philippines, Japan, or Hawaii. I had heard a lot of stories about Japan … beautiful women, cheap living, lots of good times. I put Japan down as my first choice and Hawaii as my last choice.

A month later I landed in Hawaii, the Naval Ammunition Depot, West Lock, Oahu, which from an island standpoint was the end of the earth—situated in a remote area at the back of the sugar cane fields. Sometime later I was advised to always put my last choice first because, inevitably, I would not be assigned to my first choice. An important lesson learned.

On my first liberty, I bummed a ride off of someone and headed straight for Waikiki Beach. Things began to look a bit brighter—bikinis … lots of them, as well as palm trees, clear water, and cold beer. But my paycheck didn't quite match my expensive surroundings. I needed a plan. How does a person without wheels survive on eighty dollars a month in this pricey place?

My first order of business was to supplement my salary. A position as a night bartender opened up at the base enlisted club. The job paid $1.50 an hour. Because of my college exploits and delayed entry into the navy, I was older than most young sailors. The successful applicant had to be over twenty-one to serve alcohol. That was me.

Stage two of the plan was to stay on base for two months. The navy would provide me with chow and a place to sleep; I would work at the club on off-duty hours and then search for a vehicle.

WWII $200 Jeep. Diving in Hawaii and "wheels" for Waikiki

Bulletin boards abound in the navy. They are everywhere … at the Navy Exchange, the Commissary, the Enlisted Club, the barracks, everywhere. In Hawaii, when sailors either got transferred or had enough of Waikiki, they looked for a quick auto sale—usually pennies on the dollar—and they always posted these items on the bulletin boards. One day I saw it: a 1943 World War II jeep selling for $200. A deal was struck, and I gained control of my island movements.

Next, I learned that I could not apply for diving school until I had completed twenty-four months at my command, so I decided to make the best of my next two years in Hawaii, and part of that meant meeting girls.

I was a simple farm boy with limited sexual experience, and I was raised to be an upstanding Catholic. It had been drummed into my head that any contact with a girl outside of "hello" and hand holding was a mortal sin. But more urgent physical demands began to assuage my commitment to chastity. After all, I was a sailor. Sailors didn't just hold hands. They were men of the world who defended the country and made sacrifices above and beyond the call of duty. We were expected to drink hardy and spin tales of harrowing death-defying experiences at sea. Although I hadn't been to sea yet, I was pretty good at fudging my experience and winning the lovelies' awe. After all, most of the tourist gals were from small Midwest towns, and had no experience with sailors, the "old salts." After years working on a farm, now *I* was the fox in the henhouse, and it was glorious.

In order to solve my omnipresent financial constraints, I usually employed the following method: While I nursed a seventy-five-cent beer (expensive compared to the twenty cents they charged on base) and talked to tourists, I would say something like, "Gee, I'd really like to buy you a beer, but the navy pays me a meager salary." The tourist's response (usually WWII vets) was, "Bartender, set this boy up with a cold one and give him another after that on my tab." It worked every time. Was it dishonest? Absolutely not. In fact, I figured these gents were on vacation and that it was my duty to provide them with an opportunity to relive their youths for the price of a beer or two. This was also the only way to survive for long at the Hau Tree Beach Bar at the Hilton Hawaiian Village.

The time passed rather quickly. I was promoted to third-class petty officer, made great friendships, went diving in the crystal-clear Hawaiian waters, and met a breed of navy guys that, at the time, was little known—Navy EOD (Explosive Ordnance Disposal). I believed these EOD guys were genuinely scary people. They were qualified to disarm bombs, mines, torpedoes, and booby traps; blow things up; and render safe any piece or ordnance ... from a cannonball to a nuclear weapon. They were navy divers, and they helped me see the connection between my mineman rating and my diving aspirations.

However, the navy did not see the connection the way EOD guys did. It turned out that mineman, which seemed like a good rating for a diver, was not one of the designations generally allowed into deep sea diving school, and diving school was where I needed to go. I applied for and received a waiver. My orders came through for diver second-class training in San Diego, California. This was it ... Mark V.

CHAPTER FOUR

REALIZING YOUR DREAMS

"If one advances confidently in the direction of his dreams, and
endeavors to live the life which he has imagined, he will
meet with a success unexpected in common hours."
—Henry David Thoreau

D ay one indoctrination of class 6908 at the Pier 5 barge, 32nd
Street Naval Base, San Diego, California:
"You lowlife, scum, fleet sailor, non-diver piece of crap. Whatever in your wildest dreams made you believe that you could possibly
be one of us, the pride of the fleet, a U. S. Navy deep sea diver? And *you*
(shouted in my face), what the hell kind of rate is that on your arm?"

"Mineman, Chief."

"You don't belong here. Whose ass did you kiss to get here? You
belong with EOD. I'm going to make it a point to flunk you out *first!*"

So much for keeping a low profile.

I said to myself, "Throw it at me. I'm ready." And I thought I *was*
ready. After all, I passed the screening test (runs, swims, pull-ups, and
more) and the oxygen tolerance test in the recompression chamber at
Pearl Harbor, and I knew *all about* the Mark V. The one difference that
was not known to me at the time was that there was the Telford Mark V
way and the Navy Mark V way. In San Diego where I was, there was only
one way—the Navy way.

In the 1960s there were no rules that addressed the physical and mental approaches the instructors used while they trained navy divers. That is to say, you were basically at their mercy. Whatever they conjured up was the order of the day. The only thing in print that was strictly adhered to was the *U. S. Navy Diving Manual* ... the diver's bible.

The first four-week scuba training was the weeding-out phase. Run, do calisthenics, run, swim, run, and run some more. Trainees never walked anywhere. We ran to breakfast, ran back, threw up, ran to lunch, ran back, and threw up again. We ran to jump in the water. We swam, ran back to the barge, and ran back to the barracks. By the way, we always performed all of this with our buddy. We *never, ever* separated from our buddy. That would have been the mortal sin of all mortal sins, and both buddies would have paid dearly for it. I ate, ran, swam, sweated, and dived with my buddy. I, for one, was happy that I did not have to sleep with him because he was ugly and not my type. I would have drawn the line right there.

Throughout scuba training the uniform of the day was UDT (underwater demolition team) trunks that rubbed our crotches raw, and navy duck feet (flippers). We held a mask and duck feet in one hand and held our buddy's arm with the other. In addition, the infamous KA-BAR knife in a scabbard was mounted to our waists on a web belt. While we ran, the knife invariably found its way to the front position, between our legs, and attempted to beat our testicles to a pulp. And all the while we had someone screaming in our ear that "pain is weakness leaving your bodies," or some other hackneyed yet motivating words of wisdom.

The runs, crawls, swims, pushups, sit-ups, and other forms of conditioning (torture) cut the class almost in half by the end of the first week. The chief was on me more than ever. If he gave me twenty pushups, I did forty—just to piss him off. I was developing my own brand of reverse psychology. He used to laugh sardonically and say, "I'm not done yet, Mineman. I'll get you on Harassment Day. You'll see." It became a personal thing between the chief and me.

Then it arrived: Harassment Day. This was the make-it-or-break-it day, the last day of basic scuba training. The objective was to see if any of us would panic under extremely arduous underwater conditions. Today we would try to put a positive spin on Harassment Day by calling it "confidence-building day." But back then, before political correctness, we were considered raw meat, and in our minds, Harassment Day was synonymous with death. We had heard horror stories from the senior class. They made it very clear that we should give our souls to God because our asses belonged to the "sharks"—the instructors.

It started with a five-mile run around the base ending at the twelve-foot-deep indoor swimming pool, which is where our first phase of training had taken place.

"Line up. Prepare to scale the tower."

This involved climbing up a ten-foot tower carrying our double scuba tanks in one hand while managing our duck feet, masks, weight belts, KA-BARs, and regulators with the other. We wished that God had afforded us a third arm and hand. Our objective was to jump from the tower with all our gear in our hands, install the regulator on the tanks underwater, start breathing, don our duck feet, put our masks on our heads, clear the masks of water, attach our weight belts and KA-BARs, harness the tanks, and start swimming in circles. We were supposed to do all of this while, at the same time, we held on to our buddies, first with our legs and then with our arm.

Before I made my jump, I hollered in smart-ass defiance to the chief, "Hey, Chief, when in the hell am I ever going to do a stupid thing like this in the fleet?"

Without a second's hesitation, the chief screamed, "Jump, you sorry son-of-a-bitch. I'm here to kill you."

As you will read later, this exchange paid dividends.

Next came the real fun. After the class was assembled, out came the "sharks." They approached from all directions, ripping and tearing at us and our gear. Masks were torn off (we had been trained to breathe with our noses exposed to water), air was turned off, duck feet were yanked off, regulator hoses were ripped to shreds, harness straps to tanks were disconnected and tied in knots, and weight belts were strewn about. It was total pandemonium.

The significance of the buddy business became imminently clear ...
he had air and I didn't. With arms, legs, and gear everywhere, we "buddy
breathed" and began to put things back together. Then, as soon as we
were almost back in commission, they hit us again ... and again. If we
had surfaced before we had both run out of air from both sets of tanks,
we would have received orders by the end of the day that cut us back to
the fleet as non-divers.

Those of us who survived this chaos were qualified to make an
open ocean dive at a later date. On the way back to the barge, we sang
in cadence and ran proudly—very proudly: "6908, tell me, what's your
line? Deep sea diver and its mighty fine!" The ensuing scuba training
encompassed two more weeks of nuts-and-bolts projects in the bay. Next
came the surface-supplied "Jack Browne," a lightweight rig, and finally
the coveted Mark V deep sea rig.

Graduation was special, and it was followed by a hell of a party. The
sign for our class photo read "As good as we are, it's hard to be humble."
But the most important thing was that I became part of an exclusive family. To borrow an applicable phrase, "Solid family is an emotional basis
for personal identity."

CHAPTER FIVE

VIETNAM TOUR—CONTINUING EDUCATION

*"The problem with experience is that you generally
get the test before you get the lesson."*
–Mike Cattolico

For the most part, the above quote about learning life lessons through experience is true. Although sometimes—very seldom—a person gets plain, old lucky. Luck should be confined to gambling casinos. I prefer to use the word "fortunate." For example, we are fortunate in the USA to have a myriad of opportunities at our disposal. When we combine that good fortune with destiny, desire, hard work, imagination, and a "don't-quit" attitude, we have a basic formula for success. After I graduated from diving school, success was my primary objective; it was the philosophy I incorporated while I carried out my ensuing orders and my service in Vietnam.

After completing my diving school, my orders read "Harbor Clearance Unit-One, Philippines." I had heard a lot about the Philippines but not much about HCU-1. As it turned out, HCU-1 had been commissioned as a combat salvage unit; subsequently it developed into one of the biggest salvage outfits in the world.

Within about a week of leaving San Diego, I landed at Clark Air Force Base in the Philippine Islands (P.I.). I was wearing navy dress blues, and the heat and humidity were beyond description. I did not know where I was going, so I showed my orders to an officer at the terminal. He said, "Oh, you need to catch the Victory Bus to the Subic Bay Naval Base. Got any pesos?"

"What are pesos?" I asked.

"You know. Philippine money."

"No, sir."

He handed me a ten-peso bill and said, "Give this to the bus driver over there and he'll take you to Subic." I thought he was being very generous, but later I learned that ten pesos was about ninety cents in U. S. currency. The officer was a good Samaritan but not a great Samaritan.

Victory Bus was a bus line that was owned and operated by Filipinos who carted people around the islands. I arrived in February, which meant rain and mud. After I hopped aboard the bus and paid my pesos, off we went. Two hours later, the other passengers and I heard an announcement from the driver in Tagalog (the local tongue) and English: "Everybody off."

"Thank God we're there," I thought.

While I was sitting on my sea bag in a puddle of sweat and sharing the space with chickens and pigs, I asked the driver, "This Subic Bay?"

"No, GI. Subic Bay another two hours. This halfway piss stop."

Then the little guy in the back of my mind said, "Pain is weakness leaving your body." I was getting to dislike this little guy more and more.

Finally we reached Subic Bay's Main Gate. I must have looked like fresh meat because several Filipinos approached me to exchange greenbacks for pesos. I had heard about this illegal method of black-market trading and how a participant could wind up in jail, if caught. At that point I was in a real pickle. I didn't speak the language, and none of the Filipinos understood my high school French. I didn't know where I was headed, but jail seemed to be a real possibility.

From out of the blue a young naval officer appeared and asked, "Got a problem, Sailor?" I explained my predicament. He handed me fifty centavos (about four cents) and said, "Take that Blalock Base taxi, give the driver the fifty centavos, and tell him to take you to HCU-1."

Saved! Never in my short career had I been so happy to set foot on a naval vessel.

The first-class petty officer on the quarterdeck shook my hand, took my orders, remarked how much they needed divers, and directed me below to my air-conditioned bunk space. Compared with the heat and humidity of the recent four-hour bus ride, this place was heaven! And this was where I met Mac (Dennis Mc Knight), second-class engineman, second-class diver, and the guy who would become my best friend and later save my life in Vietnam.

At chow (mealtime) the next morning I spoke with other divers who told me that a new team was being formed—Team Five—and they needed divers. They asked if I was interested. I thought, "Here I am a FNG (f... ing new guy), and I am already an integral part of a new team. I was then introduced to my first OIC (officer in charge), Mr. J. Right away he struck me as being on the stuffy side. Without so much as a handshake, he sarcastically told me to get rid of my stateside green uniforms, which had my name and "U.S. Navy" stenciled in white over each breast pocket. "You'll make a good target wearing that, Sailor."

"No problem, sir. Done." I replied.

Within five days we landed in Saigon, the Republic of Vietnam. We then transited to Cat Lo, HCU-1's base. Air conditioning was nonexistent, and we were stuffed into a small area on a medium-lift craft. The base did not offer much in the line of comfort, but it could have been worse. In fact, it did get worse.

After completing several small operations in which we salvaged helicopters, small riverboats, and the like, the *big assignment* came down. A sixty-ton Tango boat was mined and sunk in the Ben Tre River, Ben Tre Province, in the bad guy's territory in the Hue Minh forest

Transiting the Ben Tre River (Author)

called the Delta. This was "Charlie's" (Viet Cong and North Vietnamese army [NVA]) stomping grounds. As we said to each other when things looked dangerous, "This mission is bad ju-ju."

Duke Long—a first-class petty officer, first-class diver, and my sea-daddy (a navy version of a rabbi or protective big brother)—and I were told to fly out in a helo (helicopter) and survey the wreck to determine what it would take to salvage it. Duke was the man—he was Mr. Salvage.

Duke motioned to the helo pilot to set us down on the riverbank. The pilot yelled, "No dice. Too hot to land. I'll hover. Saddle up and jump."

"But what if we miss the wreck?" we asked. "Look at the currents running in the river!"

The pilot pointed north and hollered back, "Saigon is that way."

Remember the chief at the dive school and the ten-foot tower? On Harassment Day I had defiantly asked him when we were ever going to do a stupid thing like this, and his response had been, "Jump, you sorry son-of-a-bitch. I'm here to kill you," which meant "I'm here to save you." The chief was right. Chiefs are always right.

The helo pilot yelled, "I'll be back in two hours to pick you up … if you're still here."

Thanks, Buddy.

Somehow, thanks to divine providence, we hit the wreck and hung on. Then we *blindly* dived. (Divers cannot see *anything* in the rivers of Vietnam. Everything is done by feel). Sure enough, there was a *big hole* in the side of the sunken craft. Two men could have easily fit in it. And there was jagged metal everywhere that could have cut us to pieces.

Most riverboats in Vietnam were top heavy because they had bar armor all over the topside to prevent B-40 rockets from penetrating the skin of the boat. So when one of these riverboats sank, they generally sank upside down. This phenomenon increased the difficulty of salvage. The super structure was stuck in the mud bottom, and when we reached the craft, our mental bearings were 180 degrees off. This challenge applied an entirely different dynamic to an already difficult job.

Duke and I soon became oriented to the position and location of things underwater and developed a picture in our minds. It helped to see a similar craft upright to give us a picture of what it should have been but now was not.

Finally, the helo jockey returned, picked us up, and we returned to Cat Lo. Upon my return, I was grilled by the "brass" about what I thought of the situation. Imagine that … little me, Farmer Mike, talking to the heavies. Back in those days, relatively junior enlisted men were given a great deal of responsibility, and I was proud that I was assigned a key role in the final decision making. Once again, I felt like I was an important part of a solid family and the brotherhood.

The decision was made to raise the craft, and I was going to be part of the plan. Team 5—go! Into the Delta filed groups of riverine salvage craft, personnel, beaucoup (French for "a lot") machinery, and a contingent of South Vietnamese support guys—our allies.

En route to the salvage site, about halfway to the wreck, we were to hook up with another cadre of support. Our landmarks were some charcoal kilns and a small village on the west side of the river. Upon arrival, we beached our craft on the riverbank, which was normal operation for flat-bottom boats.

Ben Tre halfway point (Charcoal Kilns)

While Mr. "J" (our not-so-well-liked officer in charge) was doing his officer stuff, I decided to meet some of the local folk in the village. I didn't speak any Vietnamese at this point, but knew that the French had been occupying the country for some time, so I thought I'd try out my three years of high school and college French. It worked out okay because the older Vietnamese spoke French. I broke out some dong (Vietnamese money) and enjoyed some Ba Moui Ba "33" Viet beer. It was warm and awful, but it was beer.

At this point I thought it was best to return to the craft to see how things were progressing. An irate lieutenant greeted me with, "Where the hell have *you* been?"

"Public relations, sir," I replied.

He followed my response with a lecture about the possibility of bad guys being in the village, and so on and so forth. That's when I knew that he and I weren't going to have a good relationship. I began to understand one of the sayings back at Cat lo: "We are the unwilling led by the unqualified to do the unnecessary for the ungrateful." His next order to me was, "Get your dumb ass in the boat, and do not get out of my sight."

"Aye, sir," was all I could say.

As time moved on and we approached the wreck site, we realized that there was something strange about Mr. J. He had a noticeable twitch in his mouth, laughed when there was nothing funny, and had a habit of frequently removing his boots and socks and smelling his socks. This was weird. These were not isolated incidents … they were habitual. Therefore, in the navy tradition, he acquired the handle (nickname) "Mr. Socks" (not to his face, of course). After every order we would say something like, "Yes, sir. No, sir. Three bags full, sir." He never really knew if he was getting through to us.

If the average enlisted man didn't cotton to his OIC (officer in charge), he could, given every opportunity, drive his OIC to the verge of "dinky-dao" (Vietnamese slang for "crazy). It was an art as well as a science, and the process was working. The OIC was losing it. Every plan he came up with seemed to flop. Time was being wasted, and the higher-ups knew that "Charlie" was setting up to blow us out of the water. Even an untrained eye could sense that a dark and stormy day was on the horizon.

One day a helo mysteriously arrived, picked up "Socks," and dropped off a new LT (lieutenant). Enter Mr. Bornmann, a tall, lanky, easygoing, listen-to-the-troops kind of guy. We respectfully called him dai wi (leader). That was quite a compliment for a junior officer. Mr. B. turned out to be an ace. Everybody liked him because he had the c/s factor … common sense. He listened to the troops. Socks never did. Things started to turn around.

By then we were approaching three weeks in the bush, on the river.

This was not good. Our ears and skin sores became infected from the diving; water and food were running low. Every night got a little spookier. Even our Viet allies were getting jumpy. What used to be not-so-bad C-Rats (commuted rations—meals in a box) were beginning to taste unpalatable. Those things were good for a meal or two, but a steady stream of them was not a morale builder.

Allow me to describe the food and other items that arrived in a box dated 1963: pork and beans, ham and eggs with lima beans (can't imagine what nutritionist came up with that one), or spaghetti and meatballs (lucky you if you got more than one meatball in a can); peaches or pears in syrup; a nondescript cake; four cigarettes (usually menthol); TP (toilet paper—four small sheets); matches too old to light; one interdental stimulating device (U. S. government nomenclature for a toothpick); and the coveted P-38 can opener (a device a little larger than your thumbnail).

The P-38 was amazing when it was used by a seasoned operator who could open any can with lightning speed—faster than with any modern electric kitchen can opener. It was also a multiuse device, functional for picking off leeches, cleaning fingernails, and so on. The P-38 was always at arm's reach, usually hanging on the chain around our necks, next to our dog tags, and it was as closely guarded as our wristwatches. Somehow our P-38s and our wristwatches could disappear in the blink of an eye around our "allies."

After three weeks of C-Rats, even our allies started to go out into the jungle in search of vegetables or other culinary surprises. Some returned and some didn't … for various reasons. It didn't seem to faze them much when some of them got blown away by booby traps and the like. Those who returned brought back some interesting stuff—onions, pineapples, bananas, tomatoes, scallions, and dead monkeys

Booby Traps

"Fresh Fruit from the Garden"

and snakes. At first I thought I'd stick to the C-Rats, but when they started cooking everything together in their shallow cook pans, like a Mongolian barbecue, my perception changed. It became a question of gastric courage. The daring among us learned to close our minds, open our mouths, and eat. So when we heard "Hey, GI, you come chop-chop" (eat), we came in a hurry.

In a later chapter on Jungle Survival School I will elaborate on the things we could and could not eat. Meanwhile, suffice it to say that either we were lucky that we did not get poisoned or the allies were looking out for us so we could get them out of that God-forsaken place.

The upside-down Tango boat would not break free from the river bottom. Attempt after

8.4 Ton salvage lift balloons

"LCM8" (Duke Long) in the "crack-the-whip" procession down river

attempt we got no results. It was time to get serious and improvise. The navy byword is "When all else fails, improvise," and it was our key to ultimate success. If we couldn't right the craft, we would simply tow it upside down. We planned to attach two 8.4-ton lift salvage balloons to the stern, pump air into the balloons, stabilize the stern lift capability with a "baby giant" salvage craft A-frame,

Medevac Helo ("Duster") for the ant casualty

lift the bow with a Clyde winch on an LCM (landing craft mechanized) stern, and lift it all together.

Before orchestrating the above, we had to put first things first. We had to pull the bow around and put it in line with the tow. This required four men to carry a 500-pound Ells anchor to the riverbank and bury it for pull. As we manually lifted and hauled the anchor, one of us stepped on an anthill. He was immediately enveloped by large red ants that were stinging him to death. While ant mandibles were digging into every square inch of his body, we tried to get the guy back to the river as fast as possible so we could "de-ant" his poor, screaming, bloody mass. After the duster (medevac helo) arrived and things settled down, I began to wonder if I really was the indestructible, hairy-chested, navy diver that I thought I was. You can fight the enemy, but you can't fight the jungle. I don't know what happened to that poor guy, but he was stung awfully bad. The fire ants in Texas have nothing on those red Vietnamese devils.

After the anthill excitement, we lined up the three craft and proceeded down river. The sunken Tango got "lively" and broke free. On our way to a repair facility, we played "crack the whip" with a half-submerged sixty-ton river craft. Success … so far.

CHAPTER SIX

FIREFIGHTS, THE AFTERMATH, AND MATURITY

"Nothing in life is so exhilarating as to be shot at without result."
–Winston Churchill

THE AMBUSH

After twenty-one days of living on the river in Vietnam under primitive conditions, we were finally on our way back to a decent meal and a cold beer. We were ready to say goodbye (temporarily) to the day-after-day, night-after-night jungle "stuff" that drained our physical and mental faculties. Here is a partial list: spiders, snakes, leeches, flies and mosquitoes by the billions, fleas, lice, giant scorpions, centipedes, the "shitfish" that picked at our sores in the water, jellyfish with ten-foot tentacles, ants as big as mice, rats the size of small cats, booby traps, foot rot, crotch rot, dysentery, ear and skin infections, lack of sleep, theft by our "allies," and inability to identify who the good guys were. In addition, there was slime, goo, metal fragments that tore at our skin, the ever-present stench of rotting matter, heat, humidity, and little people with buck teeth and black pajamas who were trying to shoot our asses. What a great place to be away from. (At that point I didn't much care about ending a sentence with a preposition).

However, "Charlie," the enemy, planned our departure differently. He

Transiting to wreck site. Note bar armor on river craft (author)

was prepared to make our lives a lot more difficult than they already were. The enemy wasn't dumb. He stretched fishnets downstream—across the river and below the surface—and ably managed to tangle our crack-the-whip procession into a complete ball of confusion. Then on the morning of April 19, 1970, all hell broke loose.

Automatic weapons and rocket attacks rained in on us from every direction. It was impossible to discern where any of it was coming from because the riverbanks were so thick with jungle foliage. We were in the perfect location for an ambush. Charlie understood the terrain and made the most of that knowledge. It was a free-for-all on both sides. People dropped, people hid, and people fired … at everything. Bodies and body parts were flying in all directions.

Then I heard a familiar voice yell, "Drop the wreck." It was Duke, my sea-daddy, still in one piece. He handed me a hawser (heavy line), looked me in the face, and hollered, "Swim to the bank and tie this off to that palm tree. Tie it off with a bowline knot."

"Got it, Duke."

Splash! While I swam (no duck feet … yes jungle boots) I thought about mines, the fact that I was unarmed, and that Charlie was waiting for me on the riverbank. When was my last letter home? I continued to swim, jumped on the bank, ran,

Salvaging the wreck at Ben Tre (Author)

faced the tree, and stopped. The only way I knew how to tie a bowline was around my waist, the way we were taught in dive school as we wore a safety line for the Jack Browne rig, and that was a slip bowline. So I ran around to the back of the tree. Duke was screaming, "Tie it! Tie it!"

Somehow I managed to tie it off. I swam back to the boat, got pulled up on deck, smiled, and said, "How's that?" All Duke did was shake his head. He didn't even give me as much as a "well done." You see, Duke was a boatswain mate, the ultimate knot tier, and he knew how to tie all kinds of knots. I was a mineman—an ordnance guy.

When we finally cleared the first kill zone downstream and when all of the immediate pandemonium was over, Duke's only comment to me was, "What the hell am I going to do with you?" But he said it with a smile on his face and approval in his voice. Who could have asked for anything more?

Next I wound up on the big LCM-8 boat. Feeling exhausted, I fell asleep for a short time on a wooden pallet on the bow ramp. Suddenly I jerked awake facing aft toward the pilothouse (cox'n flat). At that point I became much more aware of what we had just been through. While trying to free myself from a ball of mosquito netting, a glazed eyeball that had no connection to a body was staring straight at me. I looked around at the carnage. There were body parts everywhere: in the well deck, on the gunwales ... everywhere. There wasn't a square foot of area that didn't have red-laced, yellowish fat tissue globules stuck to it—including me. A day went by without me eating anything. Spaghetti and meatballs just wasn't going to do it. A long draw on my canteen sufficed, thank you.

A COLD BUD AND A RING OF CHEESE

While the CO (commanding officer) and XO (executive officer) were dry and comfortable in the Philippines, we were fortunate to have an LDO (limited duty officer, former chief) as acting CO in country. His name was "Red" Thomas. Everyone had a lot of respect for Red. After the second firefight of the day, which was worse than the first, we again cleared the kill zone and headed out to the "Big Blue." I don't know why they called it that except that it was the widest river in the Delta, a place where the bad guys couldn't reach us from the bush.

Over the horizon came "Baby Giant II" with Red Thomas aboard. He pulled up alongside the "8" boat to see for himself what he already knew to be a pretty grim situation. Red was a diver. He loved his divers. To show his appreciation for what we had been through, he took good care of us. There were steaks cooking in the galley, fresh fruit, and cheese. I'll never forget that cheese—a giant block of cheese. And most of all, there was cold beer, and I mean *cold*.

Red handed me a beer, gave me a hug, and smiled. He was a full lieutenant, but we were brothers. I poured the beer into my mouth, over my head, and on my face. We all laughed as if the near-month nightmare was only that—a nightmare. But he knew what we had been through and said he was putting us in for the Silver Star. He wasn't blowing smoke. Red wasn't like that. It turned out that the CO and XO back in the Philippines got the Silver and Bronze Stars and the rest of us got the Navy Commendation with Combat V. Of all of the medals and awards I earned during my navy career, that one is my most coveted because I know what I went through to get it. Red apologized to us, but he didn't have to. We understood. Red has since passed away, but not in the minds of the navy divers who knew him.

Before the 1st Firefight—full of piss and vinegar.

EFFECTS OF COMBAT

You cannot describe combat to anyone who has not been in it. A description is simply impossible. All veterans who have been exposed to combat situations say the same thing. How can you describe the fear, anxiety, adrenalin rush, confusion, strength coming from nowhere, skin-crawling sights, deafening noise, little or no sense of direction from incoming fire, possible death at any instant,

After the firefight—eating humble pie

screams and yells, splatters of human detritus and other "unspeakables" flying about, trying to make yourself invisible, trying to organize your disorganized mind and body, and the build-up of pressure with no relief valve in sight? Combat is entropy to the nth degree. It is pure pandemonium.

Then, suddenly, it's over. You check your body for any kind of "stuff" that might have entered but not been felt during the melee. You look around at the aftermath and feel the goo stuck to you—the kind you can never wash off. But then you are suddenly ecstatic that the pieces of people you see are not part of you.

Sleep and camaraderie were the only respites we had from the effects of combat. Sometimes the sleep was good and sometimes it wasn't. War is a difficult way to mature, but it leaves an indelible, long-term mark. In a bizarre way it gives military people a new perspective on life and makes them more tolerant of and thankful for all of the things they had previously taken for granted. War alters one's focus about what's important and what isn't. Strangely enough it bolsters a sense of humor, and later, when things seem to go awry as they inevitably do, you forever hold on to the this wise, old adage: "Every day is a holiday and every meal a feast."

Firefight aftermath on the riverbank.

COMMANDER
UNITED STATES NAVAL FORCES
VIETNAM

The Secretary of the Navy takes pleasure in presenting the Navy Commendation Medal to

MICHAEL A. CATTOLICO
MINEMAN THIRD CLASS
UNITED STATES NAVY

for service as set forth in the following

CITATION

"For meritorious achievement while serving with friendly foreign forces engaged in armed conflict against the North Vietnamese and Viet Cong communist aggressors in the Republic of Vietnam from 30 March to 19 April 1970. During that period, Petty Officer CATTOLICO served with Harbor Clearance Unit One, Team Five, engaged in the salvage of a river assault craft which had been sunk as a result of enemy action on the Ben Tre river. Despite the possibility of enemy waterborne mines and booby traps, he made repeated dives in the hazardous current and tidal conditions, and worked tirelessly to ready the sunken craft for salvage. After raising the craft, the salvage units proceeded to a repair facility. While transiting the Ben Tre river, the boats suddenly came under enemy automatic weapons and rocket attack. Returning the enemy fire, Petty Officer CATTOLICO assisted in suppressing the attack. The units then proceeded further downstream where they once again came under an intense enemy attack. Once again, he assisted in suppressing the enemy fire. His courageous actions were instrumental in thwarting the enemy attack and allowing the salvage unit to clear the kill zone. Petty Officer CATTOLICO's initiative, professionalism and devotion to duty reflected great credit upon himself and were in keeping with the highest traditions of the United States Naval Service."

The Combat Distinguishing Device is authorized.

For the Secretary of the Navy

J. H. King

J. H. KING, Jr.
Vice Admiral, U. S. Navy
Commander U. S. Naval Forces, Vietnam

DEPARTMENT OF THE NAVY

THIS IS TO CERTIFY THAT
THE SECRETARY OF THE NAVY HAS AWARDED THE

NAVY COMMENDATION MEDAL
(WITH COMBAT "V")

TO

MINEMAN THIRD CLASS MICHAEL A. CATTOLICO, UNITED STATES NAVY

FOR

MERITORIOUS SERVICE FROM 30 MARCH TO 19 APRIL 1970

GIVEN THIS 24TH DAY OF JULY 1970

John H. Chafee
SECRETARY OF THE NAVY

CHAPTER SEVEN

BACK AT THE RANCH—HIGH JINKS, SUSPICION, AND MISTRUST

"Don't expect anything and you'll never be disappointed."
–Eastern Indian Proverb

SETTING THE STAGE

If you are offended by off-color words, you might want to skip this part of the chapter, but if you do skip it, you'll miss a lot. Below is a short dictionary of expressions and nicknames (handles) we picked up in order to get by when we were conversing with each other and the Vietnamese populace. The expressions added flavor and humor, and they were necessary when we needed to distinguish one person from another, especially during operations with limited or no visibility.

This basic colloquial vocabulary enabled us and the locals to somewhat identify and cope with situations when we had no interpreter in the field ... or in the bars.

Here are some Team 5 personnel nicknames:	
Jonsey	Small Boat Cox'n Jones
Bubbles	Ensign Hubble (diving officer)

Chicken Man	Dale Steele (seaman)
Rotten Robert	Bobby Moore (diver)
Piggy	Lt. Bruce Banks (diver)
Cat Man	Mike Cattolico (diver)
Socks	Mr. J. (officer in charge)
Duke	Dennis Long (diver)
Doc 1	Corpsman David Ball (diver)
Doc 2-Klep	Corpsman Klepper (diver)
Bac Si	Corpsman H. Koester (diver)
Mac 1	Dennis Mac Knight (diver)
Mac 2	Doug Milanick (diver)
Dai Wi-Mr. B.	Officer in Charge Team V Lloyd Bornmann (diver)
Davy	Dave Moore (diver)
Doc 3-CV	Corpsman Charlie Vecy (diver) (Yep, that's his real name!)
The Pig	John Searcy (diver)
Charlie, Charles, VC, Viet Cong, NVA	Bad guys

Here is some pidgin Vietnamese that we used to get by:	
Vietnamese	*American*
Dinky Dau	Crazy
Nuoc-Mam	Fish sauce (awful)
Ba Moui Ba	Vietnamese beer
Sucky-Fucky	Requires no translation
Whikey-Coke	Whiskey and Coca-Cola
Di Di Mau	Hurry up/go away
Di Di	Short for hurry up/go away

Lai Dai	Come here
Bac Si	Doctor/Corpsman
SO 1	Number one/good
Mot Chut	Number ten/bad
Nhieu Beaucoup	A lot
Saigon Tea	Shot glass of Coca-Cola
Tee-Tee	A little
Balut	Rotten duck egg
Cheap "Charie"	No good M.F.
Dung Lai	Stop
Hootch	Where you live
Short Time	One-hour sucky-fucky
Long Time	All night
Thieu Wee-Te wee	Junior officer
Trung Wee-Tu wee	One step above junior officer
Dai Wi	The man (or captain)

The following are some of the experiences that were ever present in and around Cat Lo and down the road in a town called Vung Tau.

Every bar had a name. The one just outside the base gate escapes me because we didn't spend a lot of time there, just enough time to prime our pumps on the way to Vung Tau. The most popular diver bars in Vung Tau were the Mi Mi and the Tiger. Vung Tau was unique in that it was like Casablanca. On one side were the Americans and Australians, and on the other side, the bad guys—the VC and NVA. Try to imagine this: When we were in the bush, the two sides were killing each other, but in Vung Tau, where we did our rabble-rousing while carrying weapons, we were waving to each other from across the street. I was never able to successfully explain that phenomenon in the letters I wrote home to a small Pennsylvania town.

The bars had Ba Moui Ba Beer and black-market American beer (Budweiser, Schiltz, or Carling Black Label). There were no refrigerators to keep the beer cold, but they did have stolen U.S. generators and ice machines. For a glass with a blob of ice in it, we paid about five times the price we would have paid for the same beer on base. (We were plenty smart GIs, huh?) But this bar was away from the base, and that was important to us.

Back to the beer. Everyone knows that ice is frozen water. But when we were in the Mi Mi or the Tiger, we did not stop to ask where the water came from. If we looked closely at the bottoms of our glasses during daylight hours, we could see all measure of unidentifiable contaminants. These contaminants were not from the beer; they were from the ice. But we didn't care … as long as the beer was gold and cold. No one seemed to know where Ba Moui Ba was brewed, and no one gave a hoot that the American beer contained a preservative (formaldehyde, I think) that prevented it from deteriorating while it was traveling from Milwaukee or St. Louis to a hot climate on the other side of the world. Between the contaminated ice and the preserved beer we were guaranteed to get diarrhea … and the most memorable hangovers known to man.

Once we had drunk enough beer, we became hungry, so we parted with about twenty piasters (Vietnamese money, the same as "dong") and gave it to the local shoeshine boy. There was always a shoeshine boy in the bar who polished our boots. If we told him we wanted "chow," he would disappear, go into town, pay five piasters for something that resembled a submarine sandwich, pocket fifteen piasters, and return with the chow neatly wrapped in a stolen piece of paper, which usually turned out to be a confidential military message that addressed some future operation in the Delta.

Our culinary gut bombs contained black-market ham and roast beef, lettuce, tomatoes, scallions, and so forth. It was made by an old Vietnamese lady who had a pushcart that contained all the ingredients. When we saw the pushcart during the day, we could not see the meat or other ingredients through the flies, but after the "gold and cold" at night, we were not concerned about a couple of flies! I believe that between diving in the rivers, drinking lots of contaminated beer, and eating what we called "hepatitis sandwiches," I now have built-in immune system that no germ in its right mind would ever dare to invade.

BAR GIRLS

They were everywhere. They came to the bars from the rice paddies in order to survive. Generally, they worked for the mama-san who owned the bar. Typically, they were fourteen to sixteen years old, and they quickly learned the ropes. They worked the bars for food and a small stipend that they received in piasters from the mama-san. Naturally, GIs with bucks were easy prey. The big money maker for the bar was "Saigon tea," so they had to hustle as many as possible in the shortest given time. Saigon

Saigon. Note bullet-riddled wall—author.

Tea was a shot glass of black-market Coca-Cola that cost GIs about two hundred piasters, which was around five U.S. dollars. The girls would sit on our laps, stroke our legs (and other areas), smile, and encourage the consumption of more gold and cold. We never knew what the girls were jabbering about to their cohorts, but we had an idea. We learned very quickly that they were taking us to the cleaners with their innocent

smiles. After a few episodes of financial clock-cleaning, the poor sap GIs' pockets were empty, but the sweet things continued to ask, "Pweez, you buy me one more tea. You souvenir me _ _ _."

Answer: "No, you didi mau (leave)."

"Pweez, one more?"

"No, you didi."

Then she underwent an abrupt personality change. Not so sweetly, the young girl would respond, "You … you … you cheap "Charie" … you no good GI mother fucker!"

What would come out of their mouths I would not hold in my hand … and from a little ninety-pound teenager. Some of the lessons we learned were more expensive than others.

WHERE'S JONSEY?

Mi Mi Diver Bar—Vung Tau, Vietnam 1970

One morning, after a wild day and night at the Mi Mi, everyone mustered bleary eyed and hung over for quarters at Cat Lo. All were present and accounted for—except Jonsey, the boat coxswain.

"Anybody seen Jonsey?"

We started the hunt. Finally, about mid-morning, he was discovered lying comatose in the back of the Cat Lo bar; he was covered with flies and barely breathing. He had managed to consume almost a full quart of Jack Daniels, pass out, and sleep through an attack of rats. They had chewed off flesh from his fingers, eyelids, and elbows. He never felt a thing until we managed to awaken him. The corpsmen worked on him for some time but decided that he was beyond local repair. He was medevaced to the Da Nang Medical Facility, and we never saw or heard from him again. No one left the base for a couple of days after that, but it was only a temporary deterrent for bona fide U.S. Navy blue jackets. Within a few days we headed back to the Mi Mi.

"BAC SI" (Doc) Koester

One evening at the Mi Mi, who should turn up but Socks, the twitchy officer who was mysteriously replaced in mid-tour. Why he was back, we had no idea, but we could see he was smiling and trying to be nice to us.

I approached him and said, "Hi, Mr. J. How about a cold one?" Un-

Author

beknown to him, it was payback time for us. As I wrote earlier, sailors are innately talented when it comes to screwing with the mind of someone like Socks. We decided to "nice" him to death so he would lower his guard. We got him blown out of his sneakers with shots and beer. Socks wasn't much of a drinker, so it didn't take long before he was so wasted that he lost his mouth twitch … temporarily. When he passed out on the floor, one of the boys went to rent a room at the Belair Hotel. Another picked up an old mama-san off the street and paid her well to sleep with Socks for the night. This old gal had to be in her seventies, and she showed definite signs of having been put though the ringer. She had one leg and very few teeth. Her gums and the few teeth she had were heavily stained with betel nut juice. Butt ugly!

We carted Socks to the hotel, stripped him down, threw him in bed, and instructed the old gal to stay with him until he awoke. Socks was another guy whom we never saw or heard from again.

LITTLE BOBBY

As I stated previously, every bar had at least one shoeshine boy. They could put a spit shine on liberty boots in a flash. We took a liking to them and felt that they were not going to have much of a life after we left.

Our main little guy was Bobby. I don't know what his real name was, but that's what we called him. He responded to that name like a puppy would. We figured Bobby was about ten or twelve years old. He was a real hustler, spoke pretty good broken English, and was enterprising in the way he sternly directed other kids to other bars so he could maintain his monopoly at the Mi Mi. He acted like he was the head "coolie" shoeshine boss. Although Bobby was malnourished, dirty, and ragged, he kept up the pace and never missed a beat between shinning boots and keeping us supplied with hepatitis sandwiches.

We were now occupying new hootches (housing) at Cat Lo. The SEALS had moved out, and we had taken over their accommodations. It was a definite upgrade. We adopted Bobby to live in our on-base hootch. He shined our boots, conversed with our "allies," and was generally a happy kid who enjoyed good food and a bed of his own—things he had never been able to have before. We even had little green uniforms made for him. Little Bobby was like our mascot. He was everywhere we were. We got him to bathe; the corpsman looked after his medical needs; he stood with us at quarters and made us laugh when he laughed. Bobby was a breath of fresh air when we returned from the bush.

Then one night a giant explosion interrupted the calmness. Four riverboats in a nest had been sunk at the pier, and they suffered several casualties. The invaders were Sappers—enemy swimmers. It turned out that Bobby had studied our habits very well for a period of time. He knew who was out, who was in, who was on watch, who was off, and on what days and times. When we traced back his observations and calculated his

High above Dong Tam. Note .50 caliber on the Gun Ship

sporadic (and now obvious) mysterious appearances and disappearances, we discovered—too late—what he had been doing. Bobby was an inside guy for the VC.

After we realized what Bobby had been up to, our complete mindset changed. Compassion and sympathy turned into hate and mistrust. Our senses of humor became dark, and our general attitudes and personalities became isolated and territorial. Camaraderie and the team were all that mattered. Questions surfaced as to the futility of it all.

The best thing that could have happened to us at that time did happen. We were told to saddle up for another operation. We were committed to getting the job done with whatever it took, ending our tour in one piece, and flying back to the Philippines for a taste of sanity.

Bumped from this flight.
Crashed after takeoff. Lucky me.

CHAPTER EIGHT

AN AWAKENING

"Aw, jungle's okay. If you know her you can live in her real good;
if you don't she'll take you down in an hour. Under."
–Michael Herr, Dispatches, 1977

A t the end of May, 1970, Team 5 was relieved and rotated back to the Philippines. The rotation of HCU-1 teams was a lot different than the rotation of other units in Vietnam. We were three months in and three months out. I suppose that schedule was due to the nature of our operations. Army and marine personnel, with whom we regularly came in contact, often said, "You guys are crazy. No perimeters, no fire support, no nothing. You go sit in the middle of a river for weeks. You might as well announce, 'Here we are. Come and blow us out of the water!'" I suppose they were right, but I never gave it much thought. After all, wasn't that what U.S. Navy combat salvage divers were supposed to do?

We were back in the Philippines, P.I.

*Left to Right; Author, Duke—My
Sea Daddy and Bac Si—Doc*

(navy slang for the Republic of the Philippines). The weather was hot and humid with some rain, but not as bad as what we left in Vietnam. In the Philippines we had Peewee's, a diver's bar, and the coldest San Miguel beer in town. We enjoyed music, pretty girls, good chow (on and off base), haircuts, massages, and clean civilian clothes. The money exchange at the Bank of the Philippines was thirty-five pesos and forty-five centavos for five U.S. dollars. A beer at Peewee's was fifty centavos, which was about seven cents American. If you do the math, you can figure out just how far five bucks took us. If we didn't have duty and were forced to stay on base, we were at Peewee's. During the day we worked at the unit and dived. At night, we partied hard.

Pee Wee's Diver Bar (Pilippines)

This was the life. Sometimes Mac, my buddy, and I would go off the beaten track on his Honda motorcycle to the Little Brown Jug. There the beer was twenty-five centavos. If we were still there past curfew (9 P.M. to 5 A.M.), we would pull the motorcycle into the bar and sleep on the band stage. The following morning we would return to the base in time for muster.

After about a month of this lifestyle, our routine began to take its toll. As a result, it was determined that we needed more training … small arms, demolition, advanced diving, and jungle survival.

We welcomed the training as a deviation from the monotonous norm. When sailors are bored, they begin to do stupid things, and stupid things can be costly in both money and lives. I was not immune to our boredom stupidity, so I was all for jungle survival training. Naturally, since we had all survived previously in the jungles of Vietnam, we reported for training certain that we knew it all already. Time for another lesson.

Our instructors were little, curly-haired Filipino guys, each one no more than five feet tall. They were referred to as "Negritos." They were darker skinned than the typical Filipinos and were descendants of an indigenous tribe. We learned that they had been quite effective in WWII against the Japanese. To give us an idea of their stealth capabilities, we started the training by playing a kind of hide-and-seek game. One moment the Negritos were there, and in the next instant they were gone. Then when we least expected it, we would see them standing next to one of us with a knife at a throat. It didn't take us much time to develop a healthy respect for these little guys.

Stealth was only the beginning. They were fast too. They demonstrated their ability to—now pay attention—sneak up on a *dog*, simulate cutting its throat, and disappear again. Even with dogs' superior hearing and sense of smell, these Negritos could get the drop on them. They could squat motionless for hours on end. It was as if they were machines, not humans. Since they were toddlers they had been taught these survival skills by their tribe members. They needed to know these techniques in order to stay alive in the jungle, and they were sharing their knowledge with us. I don't know what our government paid them … certainly not much … but the services we received from these people would have been cheap at a hundred times the going price.

They taught us how to use bamboo for everything imaginable … weapons, snares to catch food, booby traps, cooking tools, instruments for entertainment, and implements to provide drinking water. We learned that bamboo could do anything. They taught us how to hunt, what to eat, and how to eat. We learned that if it flies, walks, swims, or crawls, it is generally safe to eat; but if it grows, no matter how hungry you are, unless you *really* know what it is, it might very well be your last meal.

Many more lessons followed: about booby traps, how to make them *and* how to avoid them, and about when to listen and when to talk. The information they shared with us was endless and fascinating. I loved that school. I became a very attentive student and not so much of a know-it-all anymore.

After about three days of instruction, we were on our own. We were issued a small bag of rice and a machete (big knife) and then led into the bush by our instructors. Again, they vanished. This was our practical field exercise. It was up to us to make snares to catch food, boil our ration of rice (enough for a three-day stay), and generally get the feel of the jungle—the sounds, sights, mosquitoes, flies, heat, rain, and miserable living conditions.

Incidentally, we were taught never to swat a mosquito. A swat makes noise, which is bad in the bush, but more important, it drives the mosquito's proboscis into the skin, which is an invitation to malaria. So don't swat mosquitoes, swipe them instead.

At this point I was feeling like Jungle Jim, completely up to this survival thing. The Philippine jungle is almost a rubber stamp of the Vietnam jungle, the same flora and fauna (generally), the same sounds by day and night, and the same apprehensions when the sun goes down. There is one big difference though. In the Philippines no one was shooting at us.

During the day the jungle canopy was so dense that very little sun could shine through. However, one day, after I had set my snares and approached a stream to check out the crawdad population (like tiny lobsters … very good eating … just ask any Louisianan), the sun happened to be shining directly on a rather large rock sitting midstream. The water in the stream was clear and only about eighteen inches deep, and the rock was about ten feet in diameter. It looked like the perfect place to rest and while away the time, so I waded to the rock, took off my boots and UDT trunks (navy divers' traditional trunks), and laid on my back completely naked. It sure felt good—much like poolside at the Hilton Hawaiian Village—until I sensed company. I looked up and spied a rather sizeable head on an overhanging limb. The head belonged to a very, very large boa constrictor that was ready to drop down on "Jungle Jim" as he was napping.

During our indoctrination we were told that there were 100 snake species in the jungle. Ninety-nine of them were poisonous, and the other one swallowed you whole. The snake in the tree was the "swallow whole" variety. Generally the boa constrictors preyed on the wild pig population, but this guy envisioned me as a dietary deviation that would tide him over for a month or more. Snakes are not my favorite animals, not by a long shot. In fact, I *hate* snakes. As I said, those Negritos could move remarkably fast, but no one could have outrun me that day. I was living proof that navy divers not only can travel underwater, they also can run on top of the water.

Later one of my shipmates happened by and asked me what I was doing without any sign of clothes or boots. After I pointed to the man-eater, we both laughed. To this day I cannot abide snakes or spiders. They each give me the creeps.

Lots of rubber trees live in Vietnam, and rubber tree spiders live in them. I am told that the spiders are not venomous. However, they mature to the size of a dinner plate and are hideously ugly. Those of us who suffered the misfortune of having one fall on our heads or shoulders became instantly proficient in the "Charlie Brown Shuffle."

Essentially, every one of God's creations—animal, vegetable, and mineral—that could harm human beings was placed in the jungle. Maybe He put them there thinking that humans didn't belong there. After jungle survival school we were all much more aware of our jungle surroundings, certainly more so than we had been during our first tour. "Jungle Jim" and his shipmates were humbled and much better prepared for what was to come in the future.

CHAPTER NINE

THE RETURN

> "We have done so much for so long with so little,
> we can do absolutely anything forever with nothing."
> –American Serviceman's Mantra

SECOND COMBAT TOUR

As I approached my second tour in a combat zone, my attitude was substantially different from what it was when I was about to go on the first tour. This time, I did not seek excitement, thrills, glory, or medals. I was not interested in learning any more about the Vietnamese people or their country. I just wanted to do my job with pride and survive the experience.

The key to surviving a second tour in a combat zone involved making several commitments to myself. I called them my personal ten commandments:

1. You've been there once before and have done some stupid things, yet you escaped unscathed. Don't do those things again. You may not be as lucky this time.
2. No more handing out Hershey's bars to Vietnamese kids. The child you feel sorry for may just have a hand grenade in his pocket.
3. Don't piss off the bow and drink off the stern.

4. Thanks to the Negritos, you know what—and what not—to eat. Stick to their advice.
5. If you get the chance, go to Tudo Street in Saigon. It will be a lifelong experience, a lesson in history and culture without a book.
6. If you can't get something through the navy supply system that you need to perform your job, steal it. If you can't steal it, make it.
7. Don't trust anyone except your shipmates.
8. Don't drink that unidentifiable stuff at the bottom of a bottle of Ba Moui Ba beer.
9. Limit your intake of hepatitis sandwiches.
10. Keep the above nine commandments handy at all times, and remember that there are 100 more that you are keeping in your common sense memory bank. Trust yourself.

In 1968 one of the fiercest battles in the annals of the Vietnam War raged, the battle of Khe Sanh. Khe Sanh was two remote hills not far from the Cambodian border. The upshot of the battle was that the death toll on both sides was horrendous. Shortly after the U. S. Marines secured the hills and decimated the enemy, the area was abandoned. We all had heard about this event, but we could not get a straight answer as to why we left the area after sacrificing so many men.

Dennis McKnight "Mac" Engineman Second Class 1970

After our arrival at Cat Lo, when Mac and I were prepping some salvage machinery, I noticed a Tango boat high and dry "on the wall"—a term for a craft that was inoperable and awaiting repair.

"Hey, Mac, that looks like the same Tango that we were trying to raise at Ben Tre."

A closer look revealed the big hole from the VC mine on the port side. This was our former "rush job." We were told that that mission was of great expediency and importance and that, virtually, the outcome of the war hinged on us salvaging this boat in no time flat.

Mac said, "It's going to be scrapped. That was just a drill to see how our "allies" and we could coordinate in that area."

Seeing that boat started me wondering what the hell we were really doing in Vietnam. Khe Sanh, Tet '68, Ben Tre, and all the other "Priority One" ops that were previously abandoned joined together in my gut and gave me a feeling I did not like.

Shortly thereafter we were given another priority one operation, to proceed to an area in the South China Sea to raise a CCB (combat communications riverboat) that had broached and sunk while being towed to a repair facility. This was another hot one because there was supposed to be some sensitive communications gear on board. This should be an easy day's work. There were no bad guys out there in the South China Sea. Our navy owned the South China Sea, and this was the area from which our carriers launched planes for sorties "in country." This would be diving and salvage in relatively clear water, not in the mud of the rivers.

"Jack Browne" Rig

Mac and I made the first dive in surface-supplied, lightweight Jack Browne gear. For the first time in a year we could see underwater, and we were soon on the bottom at about forty feet. He grabbed my shoulders and we went mask to mask to talk to each other, which we were able to do with the Jack Browne rig.

Mac said, "Cat, you go starboard side and I'll go port to look for deck cleats to make a lift." Once again, the craft was upside down and half covered with mud. The bow was pointing to the surface. We had great visibility; it seemed just like the movies. As I was poking around, I felt Mac tap me on the shoulder. I turned and he motioned for me to follow him.

Dennis Mac, my eel buddy

Then he pointed up toward the port gunwale. As I stuck my head into the area, the biggest, greenest, and meanest saw-toothed moray eel that I had ever seen greeted me head to head. This guy would have been too big to fit into a large aquarium at Sea World. His head was the size of a football. Moray eels can ruin your day with their teeth and strength. As I backpedaled faster than I ever thought I could, I heard Mac laughing. He was laughing so hard that he broke the rubber seal on his mask, which was filling up with water.

We ascended to report the findings. When Mac and I were on deck, I slapped at him while we both laughed. Everyone on deck was intrigued as we described that monster eel. Of course, we were then harassed beyond belief by the salvage boat officers for being wimps. At that point I handed my mask and rig to the lead harasser and said, "Okay, Lieutenant. Go look for yourself." He wasn't in the water five minutes when he surfaced gasping, "Jesus, that's the biggest mother I've ever seen."

For the remainder of the day we dropped dozens of hand grenades into the water to kill, or at least drive away, that monster moray. The next day he was still there, but he had become really aggressive. Because we could not get rid of him, we had to work around him.

Hand grenades for "Mr. Moray Eel"

The lieutenant said, "Okay, Cat. You know the lay of the land, so you're the first diver in this morning."

My salvation was that I was going down in the Mark V deep sea rig, which would provide ample protection from Mr. Moray. As dangerous as they are, moray eels cannot bite through a spun copper helmet.

The plan was first to wash the mud away from the wreck with the Thomson wash-out nozzle, using high-pressure water that was fed through a 2 ½-inch "T" pipe system. This was supposed to be the ticket. After two hours of creating the biggest underwater mud storm known to mankind, the pressure was cut off.

"Red diver, (that's me) give us a progress report," came the instructions from the boat.

I felt around … mud to the right of me, mud to the left of me, mud in back of me, and mud on top of me. I had washed myself into a big, deep mud hole. Now I felt like a total incompetent.

"I hate to tell you this, guys, but I'm trapped and can't move."

After about three hours, they managed to get me out. At that point I knew what humble pie tasted like. I can take my share of ridicule, but going from "Moray Mike" to "Mr. Mud" was no promotion. Even so, I retained my sense of humor, which is always the best antidote, and Mac defended me all the while.

One new creature that I was introduced to in Vietnam was the indigenous and very venomous sea snake. We were told that although they were small, sea snakes were curious and would attack without provocation. And there was no antivenin. Worse, they were known to go up river in the Delta. Although their jaws were small, if they broke through your skin, you had about seven minutes to say as many "Our Fathers" as you could. I did see plenty of them in the South China Sea. In fact, they attacked the bubbles that were expelled from my Mark V. It was kind of eerie, but I was protected by cotton vulcanized dress and a spun-copper helmet, so I was never worried. However, a short time later I saw a Vietnamese fisherman who was bitten by a sea snake. He was dead within ten minutes.

DELONG PIER

A short distance from Cat Lo was an LST (landing ship tank) merchant ship that had suffered a fouled propeller on its port side. We were called upon to remove about fifty feet of spring-lay wire rope (cable). It was very tightly jammed around the propeller shaft, and the only way to free it was to use hacksaws, which was a painfully slow process that we had to perform piece by piece. Of course, visibility was zero, and all of our work had to be done exclusively by feel. Standard dress for the occasion was UDT trunks, green T-shirt, jungle boots, weight belt, and a Jack Browne rig.

About an hour into the hacking I felt a very painful sting on my upper left arm. By the time I ascended to the dive boat, my arm was beginning to feel numb. All I could think of was *sea snake*. As they were medevacing me to the local medical unit, the entire left side of my body became numb, and I lost control of the left side of my face. I had never been that scared before, even during my first tour's firefights, which were horrendous but fast. I believed that what was happening to be now would result in a quick death.

They laid me out on a stretcher. A doctor and corpsman were leaning over me; one was feeling my pulse and listening with a stethoscope while the other one was looking at his watch. I guess I was on my fourth or fifth "Our Father" when the doctor said, "Okay. Take him back to Cat Lo and keep an eye on him. It was probably a jellyfish." At that point I was fully conditioned and prepared to join the priesthood right after I left the navy. I thought nothing could ever frighten me that much again. I was wrong.

THE MONITOR

After my jellyfish sting recovery, the team was once again tasked to go deep into the interior of the Delta to survey a sunken monitor riverboat. The monitor weighed around fifty tons, had a forty-mm turret up forward, and a mortar pit behind the turret. Once again, it was upside down with the bow partially exposed on the riverbank. The damage to the riverboat was so severe that the decision was made to leave the boat but remove the mortar. My job was to unbolt the mortar from the pit … and hurry because Charlie was crawling all over the place.

As I positioned myself and got my bearings, things were going well except that in my haste I unfastened the last nut without realizing that it was the only thing holding the heavy mortar in place. The mortar fell on top of me and pinned me to the mud bottom. At roughly the same time I felt a large round object beside my head. Immediately my mind flashed back to Mineman A school in Charleston.

The navy had a river mine that was called the "destructor." It was detonated via an electrical decrease. If someone grabbed it, nothing happened. But if he let it go, it was all over. This was decision time for me. I could wiggle out from under the eighty-pound mortar by holding on to the mine. Then I could drag the mine to the bank to see in the light if it was a destructor. Next, I could go to plan B, whatever that might turn out to be.

When you think things can't get worse, they normally do. Unknown to me, the surface dive boat was taking fire from the bad guys, and Mac was giving me four-four-four pulls on my lifeline. A four-four-four line pull is an emergency signal meaning come up *right now*! Next I heard "thump-thump" and felt the concussion of the bad guy's mortars "walking in" on the dive boat and Monitor. With effort and strength I did not know I possessed, I frantically squirmed from beneath the mortar while holding on to the mine. Then I broke the surface and witnessed pure bedlam. Mac pulled me in fast enough to create a wake. Off we went

A zippo monitor uses one of its flame throwers to clear overgrowth from a river bank, May 1970, (US Naval Historical Center)

Monitor with bar armor, tango boat in rear

downriver. The dive boat suffered only small arms damage. No one was hurt, but I was still clinging to the "mine."

Mac said, "Hey, Cat, what you got there?"

"I thought it was a destructor, Mac. Couldn't tell in the mortar pit."

"Well, relax," said he. "Looks like an oil-soaked coconut to me."

It was.

- Handle 1: Bowline Mike
- Handle 2: Morey Mike
- Handle 3: Mr. Mud
- Handle 4: Mr. Mineman

Any more names and I would lose my true identity.

By the way, Mac, thanks again for saving my bacon.

CAMBODIA

President Nixon said that we would not go into Cambodia. I guess HCU-1 didn't get the message.

Going upriver in a CSB (combat salvage boat), the chief of the boat said, "Hey, Cat, guess where we are?"

"It all looks the same to me, Chief. Where?"

"Cambodia."

"But Chief, we're not supposed to be there, are we?"

"You heard wrong. Charlie sunk a bunch of barges, and we have to determine if they're salvageable."

Cambodia was a beautiful, lush place with high mountains. It seemed to be the type of place people would prefer to leave alone. After beach-ing the salvage craft and making an inspection dive, it was evident that Charlie was no dummy on this one either. Before sinking the barges, he had crammed them full of large thorn bushes so that we would be torn to pieces when we attempted to salvage them. It was a low-tech tactic, but very effective.

The decision was made to leave the barges. This was one of those times when simple logic determined that the application of crude, natural items defeated modern and sophisticated weaponry and machinery.

Before we left, however, we were treated to a little impromptu humor. A swift boat was traveling upriver at full speed. A pudgy navy LT in a starched, green uniform jumped off, approached our chief, and said, "Chief, why do you suppose the enemy sunk these barges?"

To paint a precise picture for you, I'll explain that the chief was of Cuban ancestry (Frank Delolivia); he spoke with a heavy accent and always had a quick comeback. We were all standing around looking ragged when Frank responded, "I dunno, Lieutenant. I guess it's because they're the bad guys and we're the good guys."

After a subtle grunt, the LT whisked off into the sunset.

That exchange was followed by scene two. We saw someone standing on a nearby hill. Soon he came tumbling down "ass over tin cup" while at the same time he was struggling with a large movie camera. He got up, wiped himself off, pointed the camera at us and yelled, "I'm from CBS. Smile."

It doesn't get any crazier than this. By then we were laughing hysterically. Suddenly, out of nowhere, a helo dropped down, picked up CBS, and disappeared. Was this supposed to be a war? Much later, after I returned to Pennsylvania, a close friend of mine said, "I could have sworn I saw you on the six o'clock news a while ago." You did, Fred. You did.

SEA FLOAT AND SOLID ANCHOR

Ca Mau Peninsula is as far south as one can go in Vietnam. It was primarily occupied by some U. S. helicopter guys and a detachment of SEALS, but Charlie always let us know that he was close by. Another nest of riverboats had been sunk, and it was time for us to take a look and evaluate

Ops with Seals, CA Mau, Peninsula

the possibility of salvage. As with most other facilities in Vietnam, living conditions were a far cry from the Hyatt Regency.

The first question we asked when we evaluated a salvage job was, "Were there any troops on board when the craft was sunk?" The reason is obvious. A salvage operation that included handling the remains of a countryman was a far more delicate operation than one that did not. The answer was no. It was explained to us that these craft had been turned over to the "allies," and that they never stayed aboard overnight.

On my first dive I felt around and grabbed a face. I don't care how accustomed or callous one becomes to combat, the shock of encountering a body underwater stops the heart. After reaching the surface, I reported the presence of a body, maybe more than one.

"Okay, Cat. Bring 'em up."

In the darkness I retraced my movements and found him. Once again, I felt his face. I swallowed hard and yanked. When I reached the surface, the smell hit the air. When the other people turned away, I looked down to discover that all I had was the head. Jesus!

People from the base, including an army lieutenant colonel, gathered out of curiosity and started throwing up everywhere. I pitched the head on the pier, got out of my rig, and said, "One less mouth to feed."

Monsoon Season, awaiting transport from CA Mau

With that, the colonel went into an absolute rage and yelled, "What planet are you people from?" He ordered us to pack up and leave immediately.

When we returned to Cat Lo, I got a royal ass chewing. I guess those boats are still there.

OTHER ADVENTURES AND DEPARTURE

That tour was replete with events and adventures: Ben Hoa and Dong Tam sapper attacks, a priest in a bunker who was scared to death and cussing like one of us (priests can do that well when scared), trading two cases of steaks and a turkey for a (stolen) jeep, appropriation of a jukebox without a phonograph needle (finding a phonograph needle in a jungle was no easy task), and Lt. B's (Dai Wi) face when I presented him with hoagies (submarine sandwiches) that I had managed to get in the middle of nowhere, and on and on.

After returning from the Ca Mau job and getting my full dose of a number one ass chewing, the assistant officer in charge at Cat Lo added, "Who in the hell do you think you are?"

My retort was, "U. S. Navy salvage diver, number one GI, team 5, sir."

"Well, number one GI, team 5, you've got forty-five minutes to pack your seabag and catch a C-130 (cargo plane in Vung Tau). You're going back to the P. I."

"Jeez, sir. Did I piss everybody off that much?"

"No, numbnuts. Your enlistment is nearly up and the CO wants to process you out in the P. I."

Then he walked around his desk, shook my hand, and said in a low tone, "We'll miss you, Cat. Good luck."

Going home. Last meal in a box (Author)
Cat Lo, Vietnam

Dai-Wi Lloyd Bornman and Author,
May 2007 Vietnam Reunion

Suddenly I felt empty. The team, Dai Wi, Mac, and the others ... I was about to lose my family. Dai Wi and Mac saw me off at Vung Tau. "We'll hook up again, Cat. You'll see."

I wept when I got aboard. I knew the chances of seeing any of them again were slim to none. But it did happen years later. To this day we call and see each other as frequently as we can.

CHAPTER TEN
NO IS NOT AN OPTION

"You can't see the view if you don't climb the mountain."
–Mike Cattolico

THE COLLEGE EXPERIENCE

When I deplaned in Philadelphia wearing my service dress blues, I saw a lot of young people demonstrating, and I received some ugly looks. Despite them, I loved my uniform and was proud to wear it.

No one was at the airport to greet me because I had not given my detailed flight info to my folks. I wanted to surprise them. As the shuttle bus approached my family's farmhouse, I saw bunting draped all over it and a big sign that read "Welcome home from Vietnam."

After Mother's tears stopped flowing and things settled down, questions came from all quarters: "Did you kill anybody?" "Tell us about your friends." "What are you going to do now?"

I totally avoided answering the first question and then told them that I was going to go back to school. Mother started to cry again. She felt that all of her ministrations and nagging had paid off and that I was finally going to be the scholar she had always dreamed of having. "He has finally seen the light," she thought.

Actually, the light I saw was in the U.S. Navy. Outside of Dai Wi and a couple of other fine officers I had served with, I was convinced deep down inside that I too had what it took to be a successful leader. After all, Mother Majella told me that I would be a leader of men, and nuns did not lie. The time had come for me to pursue that goal.

I applied to the State University of New York. They had a program that invited veterans in on a probationary basis. I would get my degree, attend Officer Candidate School, and receive a commission in the U. S. Navy.

I transferred as many credits as I could from Temple University and then had an audience with a State University of New York advisor. I told him that I was in a hurry and needed to muster a degree in one year. He looked at me blankly with a deer-in-the-headlights stare and said, "It's impossible."

There was that word again ... "*impossible.*" To me that word acts as a red cape does to a bull.

The advisor said that I could not possibly earn sixty-plus credits in one year.

"Why not?" I asked. "If I go day and night, summer and winter, there is no reason why I can't. Besides, sir, 'impossible' is like the four-letter word 'can't.' There are no such words or synonyms in my vocabulary."

He had probably not been called "sir" for at least thirty years, but he seemed to understand my determination. With an occasional shake of his head, he proceeded to outline what it would take for me to accomplish this task.

Of course there was another hurdle—money. I had saved some in the navy, but it was not nearly enough to supplement my GI bill ($156 a month). I had to cover tuition, books, food, and lodging. This was going to be a real trick. My first order of business was to find a place to live that was a little more comfortable and conducive to studying than my 1965 Plymouth Barracuda. The living space I found was the basement of a house close to the university—seventy-five dollars a month. There was room for a single cot, one table made of cinderblocks and plywood, one lamp, and a toilet. Not much heat and no shower. Penitentiary inmates had it better than I did at that time. Occasionally I was able to sneak a shower in the university gym locker room. But the space I found was good enough under the circumstances. I was not there to enjoy a vacation.

Then I canvassed the town looking for late-night and weekend work. Fortune smiled upon me when I was hired to wash pots at a local restaurant and bar called The Captain's Table. The pay wasn't great, but it took care of the used-book fees.

Then it was time to turn on the charm. I stopped at another restaurant and bar down the road, Yvonne's Restaurant. I ordered a beer and gave my short life history and sob story to Bea, the bartender. I asked her if there was anyone she knew who needed anything done because I was looking for a way to supplement my earnings and stay alive while I was going to school.

"Stop back tomorrow," she said. "I'll see what I can do."

Bartenders are like mail carriers, they know everybody. On my next visit to Yvonne's I was introduced to the owner—Yvonne herself. Yvonne was French, about sixty years old, had been a member of the French resistance against the Nazis in World War II, and was an extremely pleasant lady.

I began my greeting, after hearing her heavy accent, with "*Bonjour, Madame* (Good morning, ma'am)." She responded with "*Bonjour, Monsieur* (Good morning, sir). *Comment allez vous* (How are you)?" I felt a little uneasy with the language and apologized in English for my elementary French. She laughed and said that she loved American GIs. In fact, it was because of American GIs that she was still alive today. She said she would never forget what they had done for her and the opportunities she had been given here in the USA.

Yvonne continued, "Look, I know that you are working at the Captain's Table (her rival restaurant and bar up the road), but that's okay. You do a little spy work for me—tell me how their business is doing—and I'll save all the scrap food (leftovers) for you."

I had hit pay dirt. While I continued to keep her informed of her rival's customer base—discretely of course—I was enjoying a regular diet of warmed-over prime rib. This was not just survival. This was living! Yvonne even invited me to have bread and wine with her on Sunday mornings. This is when she educated me on details of WWII history, details that I never would have read in any history book. I was 160 pounds of curiosity, a man with a thirst for knowledge. Yvonne and I became very good friends, and my French improved. Yvonne's work ethic was a model and inspiration to me, and her sense of humor and compassion helped me a great deal when I was down. I'll never forget Yvonne.

One reason I was "down" from time to time was the attitude of the majority of the students at the university I was attending. Even back then the school had a very liberal bunch of young people who were constantly in search of and preoccupied with leisure time, drugs, and the day their daddies were going to send them more money to pursue their free ride. I did not detect in them a trace of personal pride or ethics.

Veterans like me, as well as those in wheelchairs, were immensely disliked by the student body and some staff members. We set the curve high for all of the courses we attended. We were disciplined, and we wouldn't take any crap from them, singly or as a group—and they knew it. They called us "baby killers," but mostly we ignored them and kept our attention on the more important task at hand. We had a purpose. We knew what we wanted and where we were going. We were not going to allow anything to stand in the way of our goals. We were brothers.

GRADUATION

By December 1971, I had successfully completed all required courses to earn a BA degree. And I finished in thirteen months, very close to my goal of one year. Now it was time to move on to the next step of my plan. However, at that point the following Dee Shin quote became relevant: "I never hold a grudge. As soon as I get even with the sonofabitch, I forget it."

Before I left New York, I thought it was appropriate to pay a courtesy call on my advisor—the deer-in-the-headlights guy. Unfortunately, he was unavailable the day I planned to see him. In his place was one of the advisor's graduate students who, I supposed, was tasked with answering undergrads' questions.

Allow me to describe this man: He was about my age (twenty-five-ish) and had never been exposed to anything in his life but a campus and classrooms. He had long, unkempt hair, a beard, and scraggly clothes. He wore some sort of sarong around his shoulders and beads with a peace medallion around his neck. I could smell his body odor as I entered the room.

I had dealt with the love-child attitude throughout the year and was accustomed to it by then. I was polite and addressed him courteously. I stated my name, explained the reason for my visit (completion of requisites, graduation time, and so on). The first two mistakes he made were not to establish eye contact with me or acknowledge my presence.

Anger started to build up within me, but I kept my composure. I addressed him once again and received no acknowledgement. Then it happened: Something inside me snapped, and my anger surfaced. I jumped on his desk, cleared everything off of it with my foot, grabbed his beads and beard with one hand, poked my other hand in his face and shouted, "Listen to me and listen well, you commie, pinko, faggot freak. You're going to put my diploma in this manila envelope, send it to the address on the front, and if it's not there in two days I'm personally going to come back here, look you up, unscrew your filthy head, and shit down your windpipe! Got It? You see, I'm one of those crazy Vietnam baby killers that you've been badgering all year, and I've had a belly full of you creeps. Don't even think of fucking with me!"

I left the building and hopped in the '65 Barracuda. I laughed a lot on the way home. Stage one of my mission impossible was complete.

By the way, my degree arrived the next day postmarked "special delivery." Something to be said about direct communication!

 At this point I'd like to run some statistics by you that were recently sent to me by Dai wi: For over thirty years I, and many other Vietnam veterans, seldom spoke of Vietnam, except with other veterans or in public speeches. During the past five years

I have joined the hundreds of thousands who believe it is high time the truth is told about the Vietnam War and the people who served there. It's time the American people learn that the United States military did *not* lose the war.

 The American people support the men and women who are involved in the War on Terrorism, but the mainstream media is, once again, working tirelessly to undermine our soldiers' efforts and to force an impression of a psychological loss or stalemate. We cannot stand by and let the media do to our current warriors what they did to our Vietnam warriors thirty-five years ago.

"Look deeply into my black granite face and see yourself in the reflection—your face superimposed on names. Never forget the names, the names, the names—for they hold the answer."
–Terrance Donnell (USAF, Ret)

On the next page are some interesting facts about the Vietnam War. It's not a long read, but I guarantee that it will teach you things you did not know about the war or those who served, fought, and died there. After reading these facts, please feel free to share the information with you friends, family, and associates.

VIETNAM WAR DATA

- The number of American military personnel who served on active duty during the official Vietnam era, from August 5, 1964, to May 7, 1975: 9,087,000.

- The number of Americans who served in uniform in Vietnam: 2,709,918. Veterans represented 9.7 percent of their generation.

- The number of Americans who were awarded the Medal of Honor during the Vietnam War: 240. In 1958 James Davis was the first man to die in Vietnam. He was with the 509th Radio Research Station. Davis Station in Saigon was named after him.

- The number of Americans who were killed in Vietnam: 58,148.

- The number of Americans who were severely disabled: 75,000.

- The number of Americans who were 100 percent disabled: 23,214.

- The number of American who lost limbs: 5,283.

- The number of Americans who sustained multiple amputations: 1,081.

- Of those killed, 61 percent were younger than twenty-one; 11,465 were younger than twenty; and 17,539 were married.

- The average age of men who were killed in the Vietnam War was 23.1 years. Five of the men who were killed in Vietnam were only sixteen years old. The oldest man killed was sixty-two years old.

- As of January 15, 2004, there are 1,875 Americans still unaccounted for from the Vietnam War.

- The number of Vietnamese War veterans who were honorably discharged: 97 percent. The number of Vietnam veterans who say they are glad they served: 91 percent. The number of veterans who say they would serve again, even knowing the outcome: 74 percent.

- Vietnam veterans have a lower unemployment rate than the same non-vet age groups. Vietnam veterans' personal income exceeds that of non-veterans our age by more than 18 percent.

- The number of Americans who now hold Vietnam veterans in high esteem: 87 percent.

- There is no difference in drug usage between Vietnam veterans and non-veterans of the same age group.
- Vietnam veterans are less likely to be in prison. Only one-half of one percent of Vietnam veterans have been jailed for crimes. The number of Vietnam veterans who have made successful transitions to civilian life: 85 percent. (Source: Veterans Administration Study)
- Interesting census statistics: The number of people who served in Vietnam and were still alive as of August, 19951: 713,823. During that same census count the number of Americans falsely claiming to have served "in country" was 9,492,958.
- As of the current census taken during August 2000, the surviving U. S. Vietnam veteran population estimate is 1,002,511. This is hard to believe, considering we lost nearly 711,000 between 1995 and 2000. That adds up to 390 per day. The Department of Defense Vietnam War Service Index originally reported erroneously that 2,709,918 U. S. military personnel served in-country.
- Isolated atrocities committed by American soldiers produced torrents of outrage from anti-war critics and the news media, yet communist atrocities were common, and they received hardly any media mention at all. The United States sought to minimize and prevent attacks on civilians while North Vietnam made attacks on civilians a centerpiece of its strategy.
- Americans who deliberately killed civilians received prison sentences; communists who did so received commendations. From 1957 to 1973 the National Liberation Front assassinated 36,725 Vietnamese and abducted another 58,499. The death squads focused on leaders at the village level and on anyone who improved the lives of the peasants, such as medical personnel, social workers, and school teachers. These people were systematically eliminated by Communist death squads.

COMMON MYTHS DISPELLED

Myth: Most Vietnam veterans were drafted.

Fact: Two-thirds of the soldiers who served in Vietnam were volunteers. Conversely, two-thirds of the soldiers who served in World War II were drafted. Approximately 70 percent of those killed in Vietnam were volunteers.

Myth: Suicides among Vietnam veterans range from 50,000 to 100,000, which is six to eleven times the non-Vietnam veteran population.

Fact: Mortality studies show that 9,000 is a closer estimate. The CDC Vietnam Experience Study Mortality Assessment shows that during the first five years after discharge, deaths from suicide were 1.7 times more likely among Vietnam veterans than non-Vietnam veterans. After the initial post-service period, Vietnam veterans were no more likely to commit suicide than non-Vietnam veterans. In fact, after the five years post-service period, the rate of suicides was less in the Vietnam veterans group.

Myth: Disproportionate numbers of blacks were killed in the Vietnam War.

Fact: Here is the breakdown: 86 percent of the men who died in Vietnam were Caucasians, 12.5 percent were black, and 1.2 percent were of other races. Sociologists Charles C. Moskos and John Sibley Butler, in a recently published book entitled *All That We Can Be,* said they analyzed the claim that blacks were used like cannon fodder during the Vietnam War. They report definitively that this is untrue. Black fatalities amounted to 12 percent of all Americans killed in Southeast Asia, a figure proportional to the number of blacks in the U.S. population at the time and slightly lower than the proportion of blacks in the army at the close of the war.

Myth: The Vietnam War was fought largely by the poor and un-
educated.

Fact: Servicemen who went to Vietnam from well-to-do areas
had a slightly elevated risk of dying because they were more
likely to be pilots or infantry officers. Vietnam Veterans
were the best educated forces our nation had ever sent into
combat: 79 percent had a high school education or better.

Here are statistics from the Combat Area Casualty file
(CACF) as of November 1993. The CACF is the basis for
the Vietnam Veterans Memorial (The Wall). The average
age of the 58,148 who were killed in Vietnam was 23.11
years. (Although 58,169 names are in the November 1993
database, only 58,148 have both an event date and birth
date. The event date is used instead of a declared dead date
for some of those who were listed as missing in action.) The
average age at death: total deaths-58,148, average age-23.11
years; enlisted deaths-50,274, average age-22.37 years;
officer deaths-6,598, average age-28.43 years; warrants'
deaths-1,276, average age-24.73 years; E-1 deaths-525,
average age-20.34 years; MOS11B (military occupation
specialty) deaths-18,465, average age-22.55 years).

Myth: The average age of an infantryman fighting in Vietnam was
nineteen years old.

Fact: The actual age of KIAs (killed in action) is twenty-two.
None of the enlisted grades have an average age less than
twenty years old. In comparison, the average soldier who
fought in World War II was twenty-six years old.

Myth: The Domino Theory (that a political event in one country
will cause similar events in other countries) was proven
false.

Fact: The Domino Theory was proven to be accurate. The
ASEAN (Association of Southeast Asian Nations) coun-

tries—Philippines, Indonesia, Malaysia, Singapore, and Thailand—remained free of communism because of the U.S. commitment in Vietnam. The Indonesians threw the Soviets out in 1996 because of America's commitment in Vietnam. Without that commitment, communism would have swept all the way to the Malacca Straits, which is south of Singapore and of great strategic importance to the free world. If you ask people who live in these countries who won the war in Vietnam, they have a different opinion from the American news media. The Vietnam War was the turning point for halting the spread of communism.

Myth: The fighting in Vietnam was not as intense as the fighting in World War II had been.

Fact: The average infantryman in the South Pacific during World War II saw about forty days of combat in four years. Thanks to the mobility of the helicopter, the average infantryman in Vietnam saw about 204 days of combat in one year. Out of every ten Americans who served in Vietnam, one was a casualty. Out of the 2.7 million who served, 58,148 were killed and 304,000 were wounded.

Although the percentage that died is similar to other wars, amputations or crippling wounds were 300 percent higher than in World War II. Seventy-five thousand Vietnam veterans are severely disabled. Medevac helicopters flew nearly 500,000 missions. Over 900,000 patients were airlifted. Nearly half were Americans. The average time lapse between wounding to hospitalization was less than one hour. As a result, less than one percent of all wounded Americans who survived the first twenty-four hours died.

The helicopter provided unprecedented mobility during the war. Without the helicopter it would have taken three times as many troops to secure the 800-mile border with

Cambodia and Laos. (The politicians thought the Geneva Convention of 1954 and the Geneva Accords of 1962 would secure the border.)

Myth: Kim Phuc, the nine year old Vietnamese girl who was photographed on June 8, 1972, running naked from the napalm strike near Trang Bang, was burned by Americans bombing Trang Bang. (This photo was replayed a million times on American TV.)

Fact: No American had involvement in the event near Trang Bang that burned Phan Thi Kim Phuc. The planes that were bombing near the village were VNAF (Vietnam Air Force) and were being flown by Vietnamese pilots in support of South Vietnamese troops on the ground. The Vietnamese pilot who dropped the napalm in error is currently living in the United States. Even the AP photographer who took the picture, Nick Ut, was Vietnamese. The incident in the photo took place on the second day of a three-day battle between the North Vietnamese Army (NVA), who occupied the village of Trang Bang, and the ARVN (Army of the Republic of Vietnam), who were trying to force the NVA out of the village.

Recent news media reports that an American commander ordered the air strike that burned Kim Phuc are incorrect. There were no Americans involved in any capacity. "We (Americans) had nothing to do with controlling VNAF," according to Lieutenant General (Ret) James F. Hollingsworth, the commanding general of TRAC at that time.

Also, it has been incorrectly reported that two of Kim Phuc's brothers were killed in this incident. They were both Kim's cousins, not her brothers.

Myth: The United States lost the war in Vietnam.

Fact: The American military did not lose a battle of any consequence. From a military standpoint, we had an almost unprecedented performance. General Westmoreland, quoting
Douglas Pike, a professor at the University of California at
Berkeley, calls the experience a major military defeat for
the VC and NVA. The United States did not lose the war in
Vietnam—the South Vietnamese did.

The fall of Saigon occurred on April 30, 1975, two years
after the American military left Vietnam. The last American troops departed the country in their entirety March
29, 1973. How could we have lost a war we had stopped
fighting two years previously? The Americans fought to an
agreed stalemate.

The peace settlement was signed in Paris on January 27,1973. It called for release of all U.S. prisoners,
withdrawal of U. S. forces, limitation of both sides' forces
inside South Vietnam, and commitment to a peaceful
reunification. During the fall of Saigon in April of 1975,
the 140,000 evacuees consisted almost entirely of civilians
and Vietnamese military, *not* American military running
for their lives. There were almost twice as many casualties
in Southeast Asia (primarily Cambodia) the first two years
after the 1975 fall of Saigon than there were during the ten
years the U.S. was involved in Vietnam. We can primarily
thank the American media and their undying support of
the anti-Vietnam War movement in the United States for
inaccurate reporting of *perceived* losses, assassinations, and
tortures that were visited upon Vietnamese, Laotians, and
Cambodians

As with much of the Vietnam War, the news media mis-
reported and misinterpreted the 1968 Tet Offensive. It was
reported as an overwhelming success for the communist

forces and a decided defeat for the U. S. forces. Nothing could be further from the truth. Despite initial victories by the communist forces, the Tet Offensive resulted in a major defeat of those forces. General Vo Nguyen Giap, of the People's Army of Vietnam, was the designer of the Tet Offensive. He is considered by some as ranking with Wellington, Grant, Lee, and MacArthur as a great commander. Still, militarily, the Tet Offensive was a total defeat of the communist forces on all fronts.

Ten-year-old Phan Thim Kin Phuc runs in terror from a napalms attack on her village, 1972. (TRH Pictures)

The Tet Offensive resulted in the deaths of some 45,000 NVA troops and the complete, if not total, destruction of the Viet Cong elements in South Vietnam. The organization of the Viet Cong units in the south never recovered. The Tet Offensive succeeded on only one front that consisted of the media and the political arenas. The Tet Offensive was another example of inaccurate reporting of the Vietnam War. The news media made it famous.

(Credit and research goes to Capt. Marshal Hanson, U.S.N.R [Ret]; Capt. Scott Beaton, Statistical Source.)

CHAPTER ELEVEN

PROVIDENCE, DESTINY, AND PROGRESS

*"You can take the boy out of the navy but you
can't take the navy out of the boy."*
–Anonymous

As a college graduation gift my folks bought me a wonderful, week-long vacation in St. Thomas, Virgin Islands. I did a lot of diving in the crystal-clear waters, drank island beer, and unwound while I was planning my next step, Officer Candidate School (OCS).

After things started to wind down in Vietnam, I found out that applications for officer programs were being denied and test standards were being elevated—dramatically. But that did not deter me from trying. If I took the test and failed, I would be allowed a second attempt six months later. If my second attempt produced the same results, I would have to wait another six months before I could take the test a third and final time. If I failed the test the third time, my dream of having a career as a naval officer would be dashed.

I took the test once and failed. I took it again and failed again. After my second failure I spoke with some of the applicants who had engineering degrees, and they commented that the test was, indeed, the hardest one they had ever taken. Their reaction did not bolster my spirits, especially since my bachelor of arts degree was hardly a technical one.

During this time, I was living at home and substitute teaching at a local public high school. I hated the situation I was in.

Not too far from the high school were a naval air station and a pub that was frequented by the sailors and marines. I couldn't stay away from the pub, the sailor talk, and my new buddies. I was coming home in the wee hours of the morning and living only for my Monday night meetings with the Telford Diving Unit. My relationship with my parents was taxed, and we were arguing all the time. Furthermore, I knew that they were right and I was wrong. I had to do something, and quickly. I was turning into a disaster. What happened to my OCS plan? Just this: I lived in fear of taking that test and failing it a third time.

Then one day I received a phone call. It was from a representative at the corporate office of the Atlas Powder Company of Wilmington, Delaware. He said, "We recently heard about your qualifications while you were in the navy, and we would like to talk to you."

I was willing to do anything to escape the situation at hand, so I went to Delaware and met with Atlas Powder Company. They were duly impressed with my qualifications, and I was offered a job as a "powder monkey." "Powder" is slang for explosives, and at that time Atlas Powder was second only to DuPont in manufacturing commercial explosives.

After a brief indoctrination, I was assigned to a seasoned "monkey" in New York who taught me how to load and shoot stone quarries, roadways, and mines. I was a natural with controlled explosives. The pay was exceptionally good when compared to my prior years' pay, and I was able to have my own apartment. However, there were two serious problems with the job: First, keeping my accounts happy required day after day of wining, dining, late nights, and long drives in the company car up and down New York state. New York may look small on a map, but it is a big state, and the entertainment that was required the night before a run was taking its toll on me. Second, this was hardly what I wanted to do with the rest of my life. I saw the veteran powder monkeys aging well before their times due to years of double-ended candle burning; as a result, there didn't appear to be much future in this profession.

The thought of failing the navy test for the third time was unbearable. It seemed that my bleakest and most hopeless hours were growing bleaker by the day. Even so, I believed then and believe now that providence and destiny go together like peas and carrots or Martin and Lewis. Further, I believed then and believe now that there is a reason for everything. All I could do about my current situation was to go about my business to the best of my ability. If providence and destiny meant for my life to change, I trusted that I would be in the right place at the right time.

One day I stopped for lunch outside of Syracuse, New York. I noticed two uniformed officers at the bar. I could not resist walking up and introducing myself to the lieutenants. I bought a round of beers and briefly explained my predicament. After I had told them of my combat experience, my medals, and more, one of the officers handed me his business card. As fate would have it, he was the Officer in Charge of the Syracuse Officer Recruiting Station. He asked me if I could stop by his office the next day. I was there waiting for him at 7 A.M.

When he arrived he jokingly said, "I've always heard that no matter what, you navy divers are habitually on time."

"Pride of the fleet, sir," I responded.

I enjoyed a mug of navy coffee and elaborated on my past, my education, my practical experience, and my desire to do whatever it would take to get a chance at a commission as a naval officer. I went on to explain that I was committed to the U.S. Navy as a career. The Officer in Charge listened attentively and showed a great deal of interest in me and my enthusiasm. After I had made my best personal sales pitch, he pointed to another office and said, "You need to see my personnelman, Chief Darling."

I was introduced to the chief and gave him an overview of my past, present, and hopes for the future. The chief smiled, stood up, and reached for a publication that was sitting on his bookshelf. He sat down, rummaged through a few pages and said "Ah, here it is. You know, very few people know about this."

"Know about what, Chief?"

He explained. "There is a little-known provision in the recruiting regulations that is referred to as the 'Whole Man Concept.' Essentially, it anticipates the rare situation that you have described and gives us a way to deal with it. In view of your prior military service, honorable discharge, background, education, combat experience, medals awarded, and so on, we can apply for this program. The navy allows a maximum of three applicants a year who are less than twenty-seven and a half years of age to enter OCS. We can waive the testing requirement for these men and enter them on a probationary status. If you make the grade at the Officer Training Center, Newport, Rhode Island, you will be awarded a commission as an ensign in the Naval Reserve. What happens after that is up to you."

I had never felt so saved, even when Mac was dragging me on board during that second big firefight in country.

I asked, "Can you throw me in that brier patch, Chief?"

"Well," he replied, "let me see if any slots are open. I'll give you a call in a couple of days. But I need to start working on this right now. You are twenty-seven years old, so we only have a couple of months to make the age limit."

After two days of waiting and sweating bullets, the phone rang. The chief asked, "Can you be at OCS on 20 February to class-up?"

"Chief, I can be there tomorrow!"

He laughed and said, "20 February will be fine. I'm expediting the paperwork. I have a good feeling that you'll make it. Good luck."

When I told my mother of my good fortune, she cried a lot and said that she had never seen me as unhappy as I had been after I left the navy, and she knew that I would succeed in this new direction. I will never forget Chief Darling. Once again, my faith and respect for chief petty officers soared to a new high. I was finally embarking on the career that I knew to be my destiny … service to my country as a naval officer.

I reported for duty in Newport, Rhode Island, where my first morning of training was predictable—harassment by senior candidates. Most of my company consisted of prior enlisted personnel. We became very tight, and we inwardly chuckled at many of the stupid things the senior candidates expected of us. However, there were about half a dozen newly graduated college boys who had no prior service, and they had the look of absolute fear on their faces. They stuck out like sore thumbs, wearing long, pageboy hair and horrified stares that implied "death is upon me." It was hard for the enlisted men to keep from laughing.

One of the college boys stood directly in front of me. His name was Kevin Jones, a boy from the Deep South—Shreveport, Louisiana. Sometime later, after we had become the closest of friends, he told me that when he first saw me with my flattop haircut, spit-shined Australian jungle boots, and a stern look on my face, there was only one thing on his mind: "Oh, my dear, sweet Lord Jesus, what the fuck have I gotten myself into?" When Kevin and I reminisce about his plight and how his words sounded coming from a

Kevin Jones the "Maneuvering Board Miracle Worker."

twenty-two-year-old young man with a deep southern drawl, we laugh about it to this day.

Somehow Kevin and I were quartered in the same room. After he stopped shaking and we exchanged backgrounds, I said to him, "Okay, shipmate. Here's the deal. You help me with the academics, and I'll help you understand the *real way* the navy works." We shook hands and became brothers to the end.

Destiny had struck again. Kevin was a very bright guy. Comedian Lenny Bruce once said that he could never imagine a nuclear physicist with a southern accent, but Kevin was one Southerner who had paid attention to his lessons. I learned that the same officer qualification test I had flunked twice, he had taken while sitting on a motel bed with the TV on, and he had missed only one question.

Kevin became my academic sea-daddy, and I reciprocated as best I could by educating him about what really goes on in the navy. Seamanship courses were a breeze for me but the Celestial Navigation and Maneuvering Board problems were killers. I just wasn't getting it. Kevin had patience that was worthy of the biblical Job, and he did not give up. He tried everything in his power to get me to comprehend relative motion.

I would say, "The ocean is moving, the ship is standing still, yet the ship is going somewhere? Impossible."

"No, Mike. Remember, you told me that for a U.S. Navy diver, nothing is impossible."

"Would you believe a little improbable?"

Kevin tried again and again. "Think of it this way, Mike. Here is a chair. The chair is the ship and the room is the ocean. The room is moving but the chair is not; however, the chair is going someplace with the room." God help me.

The Maneuvering Board was bad enough, but then we had to tackle Celestial Navigation as well as other courses.

After many exasperating hours, broken pencils, absolute frustration, and hand wringing, a glimmer of light shone through. The glimmer was barely enough to pass the final exam and left very little to spare. To this day I believe that the chief quartermaster instructor was looking out of the window quite a bit when Kevin and I were sitting next to each other at the exam table. I also believe that the chief could see that we both had the potential to become fine officers. That's my gut feeling. Good old Chief.

For the first six weeks of OCS, we could not leave the base or, for that matter, the OCS compound, but with a little seniority came some liberty, and we took good advantage of it. Newport is a beautiful seaport that at that time was home to the America's Cup yacht races. Also, it boasted some of the most extravagant mansions in the world. During our duty there, *The Great Gatsby* starring Robert Redford was being filmed. A couple of our classmates were rubbernecking at the film set, and they were tapped to serve as extras because of their extraordinarily short hair!

Kevin and I haunted Mac's Clam Shack, Salas Restaurant, the Black Pearl, and the Chart House. I introduced him to Carling Black Label beer, and he introduced me to Pabst Blue Ribbon, my brand of choice to this day. We met some wonderful Rhode Islanders, ate like kings, and laughed out loud.

I taught Kevin what things were really like in the fleet—whom to trust and whom to question. To this day he swears that he was miles ahead of the other junior officers when he reached his first real command. Kevin and I had a partnership that I will never forget. Our relationship was my introduction to the practice of helping others, a topic I will be addressing later.

CHAPTER TWELVE

AN HONEST DAY'S WORK FOR AN HONEST DAY'S PAY

"He is well paid that is well satisfied."
–Shakespeare

Military baby boomers who think back in time will be able to relate well to this chapter. It speaks to the reasons some people choose a military career. Keep in mind, however, that the information contained in this chapter pertains to military service thirty to forty years ago, long before my navy retirement in 1991. Surely, adjustments in pay scales and other compensation have escalated since then, and I'm not sure whether these adjustments have kept pace with monetary and perk increases in the civilian job market. When you consider the responsibilities and hazardous nature of military life, they certainly do not. I'm not whining now. I am just presenting the hard, cold facts and numbers.

Military pay is salaried, not hourly. So if we break it down by month, week, day, and hour, we can analyze it below. First, let's take combat and/ or hazard-duty pay. Combat pay is received, of course, when one is in a combat zone (i.e., when there is a chance of engaging the enemy and encountering metal flying through the air). Combat pay varies with the times. In my particular case, I earned combat pay during the Vietnam

War. As an enlisted man my combat pay over and above my enlisted base pay was $65 a month. Since combat does not occur on a strict nine-to-five schedule, the hazard of combat is compensated on a twenty-four/seven basis. This worked out to be $2.16 a day or $.09 an hour.

Military personnel who had a specialty, as I did (diver), earned hazardous-duty pay that added up to an additional $65 per month. So for performing a hazardous duty in a hazardous place, I earned an additional $.18 an hour. Of course, we must include the perks: free medical and dental, free C-rations (meals in a box), free jungle greens and boots, issued weapons and ammo, and a KA-BAR knife. Smokes were $.20 a pack when they were available, and we didn't have to put a stamp on our letters home. We just wrote "free" on the upper right-corner of the envelope. Even the letters the commanding officers wrote to parents telling them that their child "died bravely" were sent free.

Here are the numbers:

Base pay (E-4)	$120.00/month
Combat pay	$65.00/month
Diving pay	$65.00/month
Total daily rate	*$8.33/day*
Total hourly rate	*$.34/hour*

And this was all tax free. Wow!

As a junior naval officer (0-1), my base pay jumped to $798.30 a month, which was higher pay than the college boys I served with received because I had spent more time as prior enlisted. My diving pay rose to $200 a month. I was no longer in combat so I did not receive combat pay, but since no one was shooting at me, I was happy to forego the sixty-five bucks. Additionally, I received Basic Allowance for Quarters (BAQ) of $114.90 and Basic Allowance for Subsistence (BAS) of $47.88. Officers were no longer fed or housed for free. When I was given housing (i.e., a stateroom on a ship), no matter how meager it was, I gave up the BAQ. At whatever command I was assigned to, I had to contribute to the officer's mess. Rarely did I ever get by for less than $47.88 per month.

On the assumption that I was provided quarters, my rate as an ensign jumped to $32.82 a day or $1.37 an hour. Unfortunately, this was now taxable income. After taxes this broke down to about $1.17 an hour, or $10,249 a year. By the way, I no longer received free uniforms, free mail, or free food. Then, of course, I had to consider inflation. By the time I became an ensign, a beer had escalated from $.20 to $.90, a pack of smokes from $.20 to $.65, and gas to $.70 a gallon. But dental and medical were still "on the house." Why, I ask, would anyone want to choose a different career?

When I signed the contract that committed me to twenty years or more in the navy, I was promised a lifelong pension (taxed). I was also promised free medical and dental care for the rest of my life. That was not so. The military medical provider for retired personnel, Tri-Care, covers only partial expenses. Military personnel must have supplemental insurance to cover the rest (the out-of-pocket expenses). And no dental services are provided at all. As a military retiree, I am basically a fifth-rate citizen in the eyes of military health care providers. Accordingly, I must purchase a dental supplement out of pocket. By the way, supplemental coverage pays only a portion of the final cost for services. I must absorb the remainder of the total amount due. Clearly, I was not in my chosen career for the money. I was in it for the brotherhood and because it was what I loved to do.

I will not compare the above data with the pay and compensation and retirement packages of federal, state, or local government jobs. That probably would come across as sour grapes on my part; besides, I'm sure someone has already made that comparison somewhere else. Suffice to say that we each have a choice when it comes to a vocation. I think the following quote by Amelia Earhart sums it up for career military people: *Adventure is worthwhile in itself.*

I love freedom. I loved protecting our freedom. So I say to hell with pay for services rendered. I lived it and I loved it. I would do it all again for the same amount of money (or none at all)—and so would my military brothers!

CHAPTER THIRTEEN

THE DIGNITY OF HARD WORK

*"Choose the job you love, and you will never
have to work a day in your life."*
–Confucius

COLLATERAL DUTIES AND ROADBLOCKS

In June 1974 I was commissioned as an ensign in the U. S. Navy Reserve. At that time I did not understand why I was commissioned as a reservist. Soon I learned that *all* officers who are trained at OCS or through college ROTC programs are reservists. Those who graduate from the Naval Academy in Annapolis, Maryland, are commissioned as "Regular Navy" officers. Once a "Reserve" officer has served a minimum of three years, he may apply for augmentation into the Regular Navy.

While I was at OCS, I applied to return to navy diving status. That request was granted. Following communications school and surface warfare officers school in Newport, Rhode Island, and San Diego, California, respectively, I was sent to yet another diving school in Washington, D. C. As you have probably learned by now, the navy is big on schools. It appeared that previous diver training and fleet experience did not qualify me for future duty as a diving and salvage *officer*. So I spent twelve more weeks in training for things I already knew. However, I had no complaints—liberty was good, beer was cold, I was paid lots of per diem, and most of my instructors were enlisted shipmates I already knew from my time in HCU-1. Together we had a lot of laughs.

Then I received orders to USS Conserver ARS 39, a salvage ship out of Pearl Harbor. Actually, I met the ship in Japan while it was in the midst of a "cruise" (several months away from its homeport). While the Conserver performed various and sundry salvage operations, I had the opportunity to visit some interesting ports of call: Yokosuka, Japan; Kaohsiung, Taiwan; Singapore; Korea; and Guam. When the recruiters say "Join the navy and see the world," they are not giving you a hollow promise.

After we finished our salvage cruise, we returned to my old stomping grounds in Hawaii. I reunited with some locals I had befriended during my earlier duty, and I had much more fun this time around ... on an officer's pay.

As I began my job duties as an ensign, I learned two very important things: First, in the few years that I had been away from the navy, many things had changed. Things always change when the military transmogrifies from a wartime to peacetime mindset. This was the "New Navy" under the direction of Chief of Operations Admiral Elmo Zumwalt, and instead of performing operations in the jungle, I was now doing paperwork that was followed by more paperwork. Second, as an officer I was assigned what the navy calls "collateral duties." As the least senior officer aboard the Conserver, I became what we fondly called the S.L.J.O., the Shitty Little Jobs Officer.

Remember Ensign Pulver played by Jack Lemmon in the 1955 movie classic *Mister Roberts*? He was primarily assigned as a division officer, but one of his collateral duties was laundry officer. I operated much like Ensign Pulver; the executive officer usually assigned to me tasks that were to be performed under the direction of a junior officer.

I was inundated with endless and seemingly useless paperwork relating not only to my primary duty as diving officer but also to each and every one of my collateral Shitty Little Jobs. In fact, it seemed that diving was at the bottom of the Conserver's list of priorities. Its top priority for me was to learn all about "driving the ship" and to become qualified as an officer of the deck and as a combat information center officer. I flashed back to the time I spent with Kevin Jones at OCS and wondered if I had retained any of that knowledge—of the maneuvering board, celestial navigation, the proper way to order a change in speed or course, radio communications, and so on and so forth, ad infinitum.

The captain, XO (executive officer), and all of the other officers on board except one were non-divers, and they didn't have the least bit of interest in "punching holes in the water." Conversely, that was *all* I was interested in. Meanwhile, to make matters worse, while we were in Pearl Harbor, I had a front row seat watching the EOD (Explosive Ordnance Disposal) guys diving every single day.

I gave the ship-driver (surface warfare officer) my best for about eighteen months; then I approached the captain and vented my frustrations and concerns. He gave me a stern lecture about how "pigeonholing" myself into EOD would be my career downfall, and he advised me not to do anything rash. He was absolutely right. I knew that limiting myself to EOD billets would assure that I would reach a glass ceiling somewhere along the line, but I simply did not care. I had no desire to command a destroyer. I wanted to dive and help other divers advance their careers. That was my passion.

After seriously considering my options, I made the decision to pursue the EOD career track, limited though it was. This decision represented a common thread that ran throughout my career path, and it led to yet another roadblock.

IF YOU BELIEVE IN HAPPINESS, IT WILL COME

All commissioned officers are assigned a four-digit number that is referred to as a "designator." Designators ending in "5" denote reserve officers, and those ending in "0" are regular navy. A line officer (ship driver) is 1100 for regular navy and 1105 for the naval reserve. My friend Kevin Jones is color-blind, and he was not allowed to fly planes or drive ships since knowing red from green is pretty important in those endeavors. He was commissioned as a supply corps officer, and his designator was 3105. Here's the kicker: I had the wrong designator for EOD. I was listed as an

1105, and for EOD (don't ask me why), I needed to be an engineer with the designator 1405. Getting one's designator changed is no easy process, and it can take a year or more to complete. One must request a change through the Bureau of Naval Personnel, submit the request to a board for review, have an interview with a senior engineering officer, receive a positive endorsement, and then wait for the bureaucratic wheels to turn (and they normally turn very slowly).

Once again, Lady Luck seemed to be smiling down on me. While I was serving aboard Conserver, I had the great fortune to meet a lieutenant commander (LCDR) engineer by the name of Bob Bornholdt. He was on the staff of Admiral Hoffman, the senior engineer at Pearl Harbor. LCDR Bornholdt arranged for me to meet with Admiral Hoffman.

When I met with Admiral Hoffman, I was wearing my tailor-made summer uniform (tropical white, long), which consisted of white uniform pants, white shoes, white socks, and an open-collar white shirt with lieutenant(junior grade) shoulder boards. Above my left shirt pocket I wore four rows of ribbons that identified me as someone who was enlisted prior to becoming an officer and who had served in combat situations.

The admiral was a good deal shorter than I am (and I'm only five feet seven inches), and he had an uncanny likeness to the WWII cartoon character Kilroy. He was a gruff, no-nonsense naval officer. He sized me up in a heartbeat, remarked that I looked like I had walked off a recruiting poster, and then asked the big question: "Why the hell do you want to be an engineer?" I sensed immediately that the admiral would not entertain any BS or any dancing around the question. So my answer was blunt and to the point: "I don't want to be an engineer, sir, but I have to be." He grunted and I wondered if I had given the right answer.

As we continued to engage in conversation, he began to write. After about ten minutes he called in his secretary, handed her a piece of paper, and made a hand motion. (All admirals make hand motions, and each motion has a meaning. Admirals don't have to say much because their staff members understand what they mean by their hand signals.)

The secretary left the room, returned, and then handed the admiral a piece of paper. He looked at it, signed it, and said to me, "Son, you are now an engineer." He walked around his desk, handed me the letter, looked me squarely in the eye, shook my hand and said, "Now get to EOD school. You realize, don't you, that it's the second most difficult school in the U. S. Navy?" (Nuclear power school is acknowledged to be the most difficult.) I told the admiral that I did realize that.

"I'll be monitoring your progress," said the Admiral. "I have lots of friends there, and if you don't make the grade, I'll personally come to Indian Head, Maryland, and kick your ass out of the navy. Understand?"

Within a week my orders arrived. I never saw Admiral Hoffman again, but the fear of God and thoughts of him reinforced every fiber in my body to make the grade … no matter what.

YOU CAN KILL ME, BUT YOU CAN'T EAT ME

Indian Head, Maryland, was the primary location for EOD school, but we began in Huntsville, Alabama. Both locations have the propensity for hot, humid summers, and Indian Head, which is located at the eastern-most tip of Maryland, also boasts brutal winters. Since the course was to take fifty weeks to complete … that's right, fifty weeks (officer candidate school only took nineteen weeks) … EOD school students were assured they would be exposed to all of the seasons.

The first core block of instruction took place in Huntsville, Alabama, and consisted of physical training and an introduction to biological and chemical warfare techniques and disposal. After that, we were off to Indian Head.

It was not difficult to imagine the sentiment behind the bumper stickers that were prevalent around town: "Happiness is seeing Indian Head in your rearview mirror." Day after day, week after week the routine was the same: PT (physical training), classroom, field practicals, study, night study, more PT, more study, introduction to diving and underwater techniques (again), torpedoes, mines, bombs, booby traps, improvised explosive devices (IEDs), air ordnance, projectiles, and much more. Each core block was built on the previous one.

The purpose of the education was simple: Learn to identify and render safe any piece of ordnance, conventional or nuclear, foreign or domestic, from a cannonball to an ICBM (intercontinental ballistic missile), from any country in the world. Our brains and bodies were exhausted daily. The size of my class began to shrink.

Then a day of reckoning arrived. I failed a field problem and then failed the retake. I was brought before a suitability board, which is a group of officers empanelled to determine whether I should be dis-enrolled and sent back to the fleet or whether I was worth saving. I was given a choice: voluntarily dis-enroll or go back to core block day one. The stern visage of Admiral Hoffman popped into my mind. I knew that not only would he kill me … he would eat me and my career. "Set back," I said. The board couldn't believe that I was willing to suffer through it all again, but they didn't know what I had already been through to get there in the first place.

In August 1977 I was awarded the coveted EOD breast insignia. Most of the fleet looked at that breast insignia as a suicide note. But to those of us who have worn it, it is a badge of brotherhood … U.S. Navy, EOD.

As prestigious as an EOD insignia is, an old navy adage goes like this: Explosive Ordnance Disposal is a science of vague assumption based on inconclusive facts, tested by instruments of problematic accuracy, and performed by persons of doubtful reliability and questionable mentality.

CHAPTER FOURTEEN

TRIUMPHANT VICTORY

"Every achievement was once considered impossible."
–Unknown

TOO MANY IRONS IN THE FIRE

As graduation from EOD school grew nearer, occasionally I was able to visit my parents in Pennsylvania ... on weekends. It was during those visits that I rekindled a relationship with Olga, a beautiful Ukrainian gal whom I had met just before I reported for duty on the USS Conserver. I had just turned thirty-two, and most of my friends were already married ... some more than once. Running the streets was getting old to me, and the thought of settling down with someone as wonderful as Olga was appealing.

Olga and I were married after I graduated from EOD school. We drove my Corvette to California and flew to Hawaii for my first tour at EOD Mobile Unit One. I was on top of the world, and I felt as though nothing could stop us.

"Mobile Unit" meant just that. Within two weeks I was on my way to Japan as the officer in charge of team 12 for a six-month cruise aboard the aircraft carrier USS Midway CV 41 (now a museum in the San Diego Harbor).

"Lady Midway" has quite a history. It was said that there are four ways of doing things in the navy: the easy way, the hard way, the navy way, and the Midway. That's how unique she was. Her keel was originally laid as a battleship to replace one of the battlewagons sunk at Pearl Harbor. Because the end of the war in the Pacific came earlier and became a lot less bloody (for both sides) thanks to Fat Man and Little Boy, the two atomic bombs that were dropped on Japan, the Department of the Navy decided to make the USS Midway a carrier. She had a permanent four-degree list that could never be corrected, but she was always underway and seldom missed a commitment.

As with all aircraft carriers, the flight deck on the Midway was a scary place, especially at night. Very quickly we learned to train our eyes on the multicolored, battery-operated wands so that we could understand who was doing what and which way things (especially aircraft) were going. This was not taught at EOD school. We learned the ropes the same way most baby boomers learned to swim—by being thrown in. We learned fast too, primarily because of the ever-present threat of being blown off of the flight deck into the wintry Pacific waters off the coast of Korea.

Most people think that the Pacific is a warm ocean (after all, Hawaii sits in it) and the Atlantic is always cold (the Titanic hit an iceberg in it). In reality, just the opposite is true. If one of us had been blown overboard, it would have been an eighty-foot drop into icy waters. Sure, there were destroyers around whose duty it was to rescue pilots who missed the flight deck and, we assumed, wayward navy divers who fell overboard, but the chances of survival in those waters were equal to getting hit by lightning and becoming the U.S. Open tennis champion ... both in the same week.

After the cruise, my team was selected to participate in an EOD operation on Kahoolawe (pronounced Kahooalaway), an island in the Hawaiian chain. And you probably thought you knew all of the Hawaiian Islands, right? Actually, Kahoolawe is one of the eight major islands. If you include atolls and archipelagos, there are a total of 145 islands in the chain. Kahoolawe, which is located south of Maui, had been controlled by the U. S. government since 1935 and was being used as a bombing and target range for U. S. ships and aircraft. We were tasked with estimating the amount of ordnance that was buried and exposed on this 2,700-acre land mass. That included ordnance that had not yet detonated and, consequently, presented a hazard to anyone who happened to be on the island.

The admiral at Third Fleet was very concerned about the ordnance since a group of local people had held demonstrations over the use of the island. Kahoolawe was an old Hawaiian penal colony, and the locals wanted it back for the *ohana*, which means family. To exacerbate the problem, there were goats—thousands of goats—eating every piece of vegetation that was available. As a result, the island was eroding into the ocean. We can blame Captain Cook for the goat problem. On his way west, Captain Cook "discovered" Hawaii and dropped off goats (of both the billy and nanny persuasion) to ensure fresh meat upon his return. Since he dropped them off in 1778 and a goat's gestation period is ninety days, it was a wonder that the island had not sunk under the weight of the droppings.

This project turned into a full-blown political event complete with media coverage. The goat-eradication plan was criticized by the save-the-whales types; the green turtle was facing endangerment (and there may have been a few of them left on Kahoolawe); the anthropologists and archeologists were disturbed by us disturbing old burial sites; the *ohana* demonstrators were running around naked and protesting Yankee imperialism; and the media were gleefully covering the whole thing. Everyone, and I mean everyone, had an iron in the fire.

The whole thing boiled down to this: (1) Get the goats under control; (2) blow holes in the lava rock to plant trees (do trees grow in lava rock?); and (3) safeguard the green turtle eggs on the beach from U. S. Marine bulldozers. I failed to mention the Marine Corps involvement. I love the marines. They are loyal to a fault, no one salutes better. And who is more qualified to guard the gates at all of the navy bases? But trying to explain the importance of avoiding turtle eggs to a marine private who is driving a D-9 'dozer was an exercise in futility ... particularly considering that the private's primary concern was not the eggs but the un-detonated ordnance his bulldozer blade was almost certain to disturb.

Now, while all of this was going on, we were tasked with escorting the anthropologists and archeologists to keep them from digging around unexploded ordnance. Furthermore, we attempted to kindly and respectfully herd the naked *ohana* to a safe place for transport to Niihau. The only aspect of any of this that was taught in EOD school (or college or OCS, for that matter) was dealing with the ordnance, but I was a United States naval officer, and my CO said, "Just find a way, Mike."

"Aye, aye, sir."

Despite the politics and the media and the naked *ohana* (who should *not* be naked in public, if you know what I mean … maybe only their adult grandchildren), there were some upsides to all this. When we had the opportunity to do so, the diving in Smugglers Cove and the surrounding waters was exceptional. Also, we were able to conduct a survey from the beach to the ten-fathom curve (sixty feet) to get an idea of the amount of ordnance that was present and how it affected, if at all, the fish and coral populations.

We found countless langoustes (Pacific spiny lobsters) that couldn't wait to jump into our goody bags for later disposition. Black Coral, the official state gem of Hawaii, was very sought after (and not endangered at the time). Normally found at 200 feet and deeper, Black Coral was for the taking at thirty feet. The ice and beer that was flown over in pallets labeled "EOD tools" was a good addition when combined with the lobster. Only those with flag rank (admirals or generals) could fly in alcoholic beverages on military aircraft. That explains the stencils on covered pallets that read "EOD tools. Top secret. Do not expose contents to anyone but EOD personnel."

After several months of this on-again, off-again charade, most of the goats were under control, and we finally convinced the tree guys that lava rock does not support pine tree growth. The anthropologists and archeologists got tired of living a primitive life; the marines left with their bulldozers; and the *ohana* were resigned to the fact that Uncle Sam was not going to relinquish his bombing range. Back to Oahu and some relative sanity.

While I was accomplishing other tasks on neighboring islands, I made full lieutenant, augmented to regular navy (no more USNR [naval reserve] and no more 1405 engineer). I joined the new designator 1140, Special Operations Community, and began sniffing around for something unique and new in this special operations business. And I found it—marine mammals.

Just across the island of Oahu, near the north side, was a navy think tank called Naval Ocean Systems Center (NOSC.) It was run mostly by civil service personnel, but they had a small military detachment with a billet for a navy EOD lieutenant. It just happened that the guy who was filling the billet was rotating, and so was I. I was rotating from Mobile Unit One. "Okay, Flipper! Here I come!" Never in my wildest dreams did I think I would be part of any programs like these.

MAMMALS

The save-Willy-the-whale people have always been concerned that the U. S. Navy owned marine mammals for military use. Consequently, the navy played their cards cautiously. The fact of the matter was (and is) that all of the critters that were employed by the navy could not have had it any better than they did under the umbrella of caring U. S. Navy personnel.

We had Atlantic and Pacific bottlenose porpoises, beluga whales, killer whales (orcas), and quadrupeds (California sea lions). We dealt with and strictly complied with the Marine Mammal Protection Act. We meticulously chose the best food for our mammals, and we had a full-time air force veterinarian at our disposal. The mammals that were involved with our navy programs were, indeed, happy campers. For example, wouldn't you enjoy the following?

- *Free food.* Our mammals didn't have to hunt or pay for their chow, and they enjoyed an assiduously balanced and nutritional diet.
- *Free medical care.* They received professional, on-the-house, full-time medical care.
- *Work when you feel like it.* At times they let us know that they were not interested or enthusiastic about doing anything other

than resting. They growled, grunted, and squeaked to get their point across.

- *Unlimited sex.* When they wanted and as much as they wanted.
- *Unrestrained social activity.* They enjoyed playing with their friends—whenever and wherever they wanted to (and they are *very* social creatures).

When the mammals left their pens (home) to participate in some activity, they let us know when they wanted to return home and rest.

When operational commitments dictated, the mammals were flown into designated areas in SCATS (Self-Contained Animal Transports), which were giant tubs of controlled-temperature water. The mammals were gently lifted by a fleece-lined apparatus and lowered into the tub while receiving a constant spray of water over their bodies for comfort. Did you ever fly on an airline that afforded you that much luxury? In addition, they were fed and caressed throughout the entire trip. Why would any animal not want to be part of the U. S. Navy? I know of only two species on earth that live in such comfort—navy mammals and my dog.

Describing all of the exciting things that happened during this tour would constitute another book. However, there was one event that deserves mention. Since we were in the R and D (research and development) business, there was always a call for our military detachment to participate in brainstorming, which was an integral part of NOSC. In this particular case, there was a new torpedo that needed some open ocean testing. Due to the presence of squibs (small explosive detonators) and a mechanical hazard, an EOD guy was required. EOD techs were also responsible for potential mechanical hazards, in this case, the torpedo's propellers.

Here is the scenario: We had to load the torpedo on the stern (back) of the torpedo retrieval boat (TRB), put the divers underneath the boat, establish hand signals with a piece of line, drop the torpedo off the stern, have the divers watch the torpedo activate, take moving pictures of the entire evolution, recover the torpedo, and go back to the base. Sounds simple, right?

Here are the details. The torpedo was twenty-one inches in diameter and about twenty feet long (lots of weight), and it had a "mad wire" that had to be paid out. The mad wire controlled the torpedo from the surface and moved it remotely to a desired position. Okay. No problems with that. At the end of the run, the squibs activated, floatation bladders were inflated, and the torpedo floated to the surface and was retrieved.

So far everything was pretty straightforward. My dive partner was a navy civil service photographer who was going to do all the camera work. I was the observer and safety guy. The cameraman was a navy-trained scuba diver with a camera the likes of which no one had ever seen before. It was a taxpayer's nightmare.

While we were in transit to the torpedo drop point, I asked the engineers two questions: "Where are we going?" and "Can this thing do a 180-degree turn and come back on us?"

The answer to my first question: "Kawai Channel."

"Why Kawai channel?"

"It's 4,000 feet deep. Crystal-clear water. Perfect for photo clarity. Besides, we're going to activate the torpedo at thirty feet."

The answer to my second question: "No way of turning. It's got limit switches in it. Can't possibly turn."

Kawai Channel is clear all right, and it also is one of the largest breeding grounds in the world for mako sharks. But I'm a hairy-chested navy diver ... so not to worry. But like they often say, "Not so fast, buddy. Hold that thought."

The photographer and I jumped into the water, took station on the struts behind the boat's propellers, gave the "line ready ... pull" signal, and plop. In dropped the monster. Off it went. I watched it. Because of the clarity of the water, I could see the torpedo at a great distance ... turning and heading back to the boat! Without hesitating, I tapped the photographer's head and pointed at the disaster in the making. The possibilities: collision ... propellers like razors ... entanglement in the mad wire. Has anyone ever seen a professional photographer stop filming when a disaster is pending? Not on a bet! Molten volcanic lava could have been at his feet, and he would have kept on shooting.

It was time for me to grab the photographer. He pushed me off, jerked his head, hit the boat's starboard propeller, and commenced to bleed profusely like only a person with a head wound can. While he was jerking away from me, he also dropped his camera and madly descended in an attempt to retrieve it. After he caught the camera and I caught up to him, I looked at my depth gauge. We were at ninety feet. In my peripheral vision I saw silhouettes of "hungries" circling us. In keeping with the diving rules for ascent, it was going to take us ninety seconds to surface (one foot per second to avoid a potential arterial gas embolism, a bubble in the brain). Decompression—maybe—at ten feet was not in the picture.

Upon reaching the surface, I grabbed the photographer, who had dual tanks on his back and was still clutching his camera. Somehow (and I still don't know how I did it) I threw him six feet in the air and over the side of the TRB. I ripped off my flippers, climbed the ladder, and looked down to see a mako shark feeding frenzy making confetti out of my navy-issued duck feet.

By the way, the squibs didn't activate; the torpedo sank to 4,000 feet; and I was playing corpsman on the photographer's head. Then I punched out the engineer who had answered my questions. Just another navy day in paradise. The engineer never reported the physical contact. He sheepishly admitted he deserved it.

OPERATIONS, TEST, AND EVALUATIONS

I returned to Oahu and, once again, my two-year tour was up. It had been a very productive tour, though, because I had attended night and weekend classes and managed to earn a master's degree. It wasn't easy. It involved lots of "burning the midnight oil" and squeezing classes between military duties and operations.

Then my friendly detailer called and said that since I had been qualified in deep sea diving, was an EOD specialist, had been an enlisted mineman, and had top-secret clearance, I was to report to San Diego to oversee the test and evaluation of two sensitive underwater projects. Wow! This was right up my alley.

Upon reporting to my new billet, I was briefed and informed that in order for me to be able to evaluate one of the systems, I would have to undergo some additional training. Yep, more diving school. Keep in mind that I was thirty-six years old at that time, and I was going to be involved in some very technical and physically demanding diver training with other divers who were in their early twenties. That put me squarely in the role of "grandpop." Although I was in tip-top physical shape, the ten- to twelve-year age difference was considerable.

I was going to be learning the Mark II deep diving system. This system belonged to the Submarine Development Group-1 in San Diego. In preparation for this task, I underwent helium-oxygen diver training (eight weeks) in Panama City, Florida, and qualified to 300 feet. Then I was back in San Diego for twelve weeks of saturation diver training to qualify to 1,000 feet. That's right … 1,000 feet! The physical and mental requirements were challenging, to say the least.

Here is a brief overview of the training. The day began with about an hour of calisthenics—pushups, sit-ups, pull-ups, flutter kicks, body twisting, and more. Then an eight- to ten-mile run up "cardiac hill," down the road, into the town of Point Loma, on the beach, in the sand, and back to the base compound. On Thursdays we caught a break. We were dropped off a boat on the north side of the lighthouse and told to swim on our backs—arms folded on our chests, using only our duck feet—back to the base, a distance of about three miles. This exercise was not too bad … unless the tide was going out!

During classroom instruction we had to memorize every valve and associated piping arrangement. There is no room for error when you are closing and opening valves at 1,000 feet. A slip-up would be like opening a deck hatch on a submerged submarine, if possible. Without a doubt, a mistake would ruin your relationships with your shipmates.

Next we engaged in open ocean training. During this process we locked in and locked out of the deck decompression chamber (DDC) and the personnel transport capsule (PTC). We practiced drill after drill until qualification week, which took place off of San Clemente Island. There we dropped the PTC to a designated depth (very deep). Two divers locked out, performed their task, returned to the capsule, ascended, and mated back to the DDC on the ship. Sounds pretty simple, right? Actually, this evolution required flawless timing in every respect.

On my dive I was paired up with a first-class petty officer who left the capsule first and awaited my arrival. Since we had "round robin" communications with all personnel on the same circuit, I heard him report that a great white shark was milling around the capsule. As I was being dressed with my helmet, I felt a nudge. My partner was coming back in, pushing me back into the PTC. That day he proved that two men could, indeed, fit into a twenty-seven-inch diameter hatch.

When things settled down a bit, my partner told me that the monster had stared into his faceplate and that all he saw was teeth. Being the senior guy on the dive, I queried the master diver at the main control console (MCC) as to what he recommended. Master diver Bobby Cave (my favorite master in the navy), must have had a bowl of funny Frosty Pops for breakfast. His response was, "Leave the capsule, Lieutenant, and if you see him again and he looks aggressive, return to the capsule."

I replied, "Did you ever see a great white that didn't look aggressive … even in a drawing?"

"Just do it, Lieutenant. Don't wuss out on me."

"Okay, Master Chief, but paybacks are hell."

As ordered, we completed the dive, returned to the PTC, and mated with the DDC. The gigantic lumps in our throats had dissolved, and it was time to go home. Of course a lot of ribbing followed, which was normal, expected, and accepted. My qualification was complete.

The beauty of saturation diving is that the divers are "saturated" with helium and oxygen to a predetermined depth. That is, if a dive is planned to 800 feet, the divers are "pressed" to that depth for twelve hours in a dry medium (i.e., the DDC). When a diver descends to that depth in the PTC (also pressurized), he opens the hatch and sees 800 feet of ocean staring at him. Because his body is saturated to the depth (all body tissue, including bone tissue), he can stay at that depth for twelve hours, twelve days, or twelve weeks (however long) and still ascend on the same decompression table/schedule for that depth. Pretty neat, huh?

"Grandpop" completed the course of instruction and finally was ready to participate in the "spook business" by evaluating the systems and operations associated with very deep diving. Details about my deep diving and other mine countermeasure projects are, to this day, quite sensitive. Therefore, I am unable to amplify on their purpose except to say that the experience was exhilarating for three full years. Also, I was selected to the rank of lieutenant commander during this tour. Again, destiny dealt me some playable cards.

CHAPTER FIFTEEN
CAN DO, CAN'T STOP

"We are what we repeatedly do. Excellence,
then, is not an act but a habit."
–Aristotle

NUKES

Around the corner from OPTEVFOR (Operational Test and Evaluation Force) at Naval Air Station, North Island, was a building with no windows, lots of fences, barbed wire, and cameras recording from every angle. This was around the time that the terrorist threat was on the rise, and since I had previously been involved in the "spook" business, I checked out the facility and was not surprised to discover that it was a nuclear weapons training facility.

I was offered and happily accepted the billet of division head (EOD) responsible for nuclear weapons safety, security, and radiological control. Additionally, I was tasked with tackling the anti- and counter-terrorism training for the Pacific fleet. Suffice it to say the latter assignment was the most demanding and fulfilling. Again, I am limited in what I can say about that two-year tour, but I received a great deal of satisfaction by being an integral part of safeguarding many aspects of the U.S. Navy.

DIVE SCHOOL

After completing the above tour, it was getting to be wind-down time for me. Because I had been somewhat of a maverick throughout my career, I had rubbed some seniors in my community the wrong way. It was apparent that twilight time was fast approaching. I would now be accepting my final billet. I asked myself, "Why not go back to the beginning? How about becoming director of the second-class diving school, which was located in Coronado, California? How about taking the opportunity to train young minds, as others did for me when I began my navy career? How about helping young people realize their dream to be part of the "pride of the fleet"? Yes. Oh, hell yes!

Master Chief Engineman Dennis "Mac" McKnight 1989 Dive School, San Diego. Thanks for your friendship!

After some serious conversations with my detailer in Washington, D.C., who insisted that I was too qualified for the job, and after some effective pleading, I prevailed. I even overlooked comments such as, "You're a dinosaur and a forty-two-year-old fart, Mike. Why don't you just retire and make everybody happy?"

"But I can benefit young people by helping them, reassuring them, and demonstrating leadership, discipline, and role modeling."

I got the job. But I had two obstacles to overcome from the outset:

One, the guy I was relieving as director did everything in his power to look good. He didn't listen to his chiefs or the recommendations from his instructors. I was convinced that he would have pushed his son in front of a truck to make rank. As a result, the facility was in shambles. The attitude of the staff enlisted personnel was abysmal, and the quality of the graduating students was below standard. Within two months after my arrival, the student attrition rate rose from 12 percent to 21 percent. This development led to problem number two.

Two, my immediate boss was a full navy captain (a "full bird") and a non-diver who, for some reason, disliked divers immensely. I think he must have had an unsavory encounter with a diver at some point in his career. He called us a bunch of prima donnas and hooligans. Not nice. When the attrition rate doubled within the first sixty days, he was furious and had a meltdown. "What the hell are you doing? Do you know how this makes me look?" I kept my cool, and that seemed to piss him off all the more.

While I was anticipating his response, I was loaded for bear. I had uncovered an instructor's personal records of manipulated grades. I had proof that students had been retained even after negative recommendations for retention had been submitted by instructors. I discovered falsification of instructor input for dismissal and fudging on records of students' physical aptitude. There was no denying these documents. They represented the facts. My predecessor should have done jail time. Instead, he was awarded a navy commendation medal at the end of his tour.

I told the captain, "I'm here to fix this, sir; you can rely on that. I am here to ensure that every student who graduates from this place will be the pride of the fleet. And if your son aspired to be a navy diver, he'd be expected to tow the line the same as everyone else under my direction."

I waited a short time for things to calm down, and then we got to work and initiated a self-help program. On my own volition I generated enthusiasm in my staff to take pride in their abilities and creativity and to rebuild a deteriorated environment, both physically and mentally. I wanted them to be able to boast that they fixed it on their own, with no outside help or taxpayer money involved.

My staff and I set the wheels in motion. By trading and negotiating with, and "borrowing" from, other base personnel, we built new office spaces, poured concrete, erected fancy canvas and rope work, bought a computer (out of my pocket), shined up long overlooked brass, created a state-of-the-art sickbay (medical facility), and procured a new recompression chamber.

Now, shining brass is one thing, but acquisitioning a fully equipped sickbay and recompression chamber requires substantially more than

Brasso and elbow grease. Here's the story: A young doctor, a lieutenant in the medical corps, was assigned as our diving medical officer, and he reported to me. I sensed that Jim could be a resourceful guy if given the opportunity. At this time the Naval Hospital at Balboa, San Diego, was abandoning its old facility and building a new one. "Jim," I said, "I want you to go to the old hospital and talk to your buddies. Don't come back without two truckloads of medical stuff for your new place. We'll build it and you'll supply it." Young Dr. Jim did not come back with two truckloads. He came back with three. Although there was not one new piece of gear in our sickbay, medical equipment is built to last, and we had the best equipped sickbay one could imagine.

The recompression chamber required even more ingenuity. We had the same chamber on the same old LCM-8 craft back when I went through this school—way back when. Recompression chambers don't wear out like other machinery does, but common sense and the need for an upgrade dictated our request for an additional "iron doctor" for the newly constructed chamber room. If we had two recompression chambers, we could train students at the pool while the boat was out at sea. As it was, pool training was curtailed when the boat was out because the one chamber we had needed to be available in case of a diving accident at the pool. But every time I brought up the subject, the answer was a resounding *no!*

"All these years we've managed with one chamber. Now you want two? *No!* Besides, it's too costly."

"What money value do you put on a life, sir?"

"*No!*"

Because we were the second largest deep sea diver training facility in the free world, none of this made sense to me. Yet the cost concerns were real. At that time a recompression chamber (double lock with two independent spaces) that had all the associated compressors and equipment cost about $400,000.

It was time to visit my buddies at EDU (Experimental Diving Unit) in Panama City, Florida. They had a department that fabricated recompression chambers. After many phone calls, visits, and a lot of pleading, I managed to break the ice with EDU's commanding officer. I hoped I was making progress with my bowing, scraping, begging, and sniveling. One day while I was visiting, the commanding officer rose from his desk and started to leave the room. I asked, "Where are you going, Captain?" He said, "I'm going to the head (bathroom); do you mind?" Immediately I seized the opportunity and replied, "If I hold it for you, will you build me a chamber?"

He shook his head, returned to his desk, lifted the phone, pushed a button, and said to his chief civilian engineer, Jim McCarthy, "Build this guy a goddamn chamber and get him out of my hair." Then he turned to me and said, "How's that?"

"Perfect, Captain. Thank you, sir. Do I still have to hold it for you?" He left for the head shaking his head and trying to hide a smile.

Next came the real trick. The chamber was going to cost $90,000. That was a better deal than we were ever going to see anywhere else—even at Walmart—but where was I going to get ninety grand? I knew damn right well that my boss, Captain *No*, wasn't going to spring for it. For that matter, if he had had any idea what I was up to, he would have died of apoplexy … immediately after bringing me up on charges. Maybe that could be a way of getting rid of him. Nah. I'd still be up on the charges.

I set up an appointment to visit the boss, the supervisor of navy diving and salvage, in Washington, D.C.—"Black Bart" himself. From time to time throughout the years Captain Bartholomew (known by all navy divers as Black Bart) and I had tipped a beer together. I knew he had the bucks; all he had to do to make it happen was wave his magic wand. After lunch we shared a fine cigar that I brought along (Black Bart loved Macanudos). He laughed at my audacity and not only sprang for the money but also paid for the installation and certification (all shore-based chambers in the navy must be certified prior to use by the Navy Facilities Systems Command).

There was only one small problem left to solve. How was I going to get the iron beast from Panama City, Florida, to San Diego, California? By a stroke of luck and the timely and judicious change of ownership of some honey-baked hams and turkeys, my storekeeper was able to coerce some naval flight reservists who needed flight time on weekends. Arrangements were made, turkeys and hams were appropriately distributed to the flight officers and crews, and *presto chango*, the chamber appeared at Naval Air Station, North Island, San Diego. After we surrendered a couple more hams, the Seabees trucked it down to the dive school.

The navy supply system is intricate and awesome in its efficiency and size. It lives on documentation, but more is accomplished for the fleet without the benefit of a paper trail … more than even the most larcenous among us could imagine. It has always been this way, and without "cumshaw," the navy slang term for such transactions, I believe the readiness of our forces would have been severely compromised. Furthermore, I suspect that in his heart of hearts, the commanding officer of the United States navy supply system, a two star admiral, would have agreed with me.

All of these changes—new office spaces, medical facility, chamber, and so on—were generating a new feeling of personal pride throughout the school, in both the instructors and students. I hung a new sign over the facility's main entry. It read "Through these portals walk the finest Navy Divers in the world."

Next it was time for me to concentrate on the diving students. Every morning I mustered the men while dressed in an impeccable uniform, spit-shined boots, starched cover (hat), starched green shirt, and blindingly shined brass devices on my collars.

"You're all a bunch of wannabes," I'd say.

" No, sir, we're gonnabes!"

"You're just a bunch of sorry-assed son-of-a-bitches who can't hold a candle to this old man, and this old man is going to take you out to PT (physical training) and PT you until your dicks are in the dirt."

They responded with some moans and groans, but they suited up for the challenge.

Look to your right and look to your left," I said. "Those sorry bastards won't graduate. Pain is just weakness leaving your body. No pain, no gain. Now suck it up!"

I think I learned that sentiment in a psychology class somewhere, but psychology was only one small aspect of my job. Leadership and command presence were the keys. I had to engender a positive attitude and purvey that attitude—can do, can't stop.

"If you quit this, you'll quit everything else in your life."

Down deep inside I knew that some of the students would not make it. But I tried everything in my power to encourage even those who were borderline to succeed. I stressed attitude and desire, the basic key elements of success. "Don't let me down, and don't let yourself and your shipmates down." We were dealing with survival under the most adverse conditions, and leadership was everything. The students needed to learn to follow my lead.

Knowing that each student had a rotating cleaning station at the end of each day and that at some point in time each one of my students would have to clean my office, I hung up on the walls around my desk just about every award, citation, class photo, and graduation certificate I had received throughout my career. This included enlisted and commission acknowledgements. I wanted the students to know that I wasn't just another officer blowing smoke. I wanted them to know that I was dead serious about success in every endeavor.

At quarters one morning one of the students raised his hand and said, "Sir, I was cleaning your office yesterday, and I looked at all of the stuff on your walls. Man, you've been on both sides of the fence!" Another voice in the crowd exclaimed, "Shit, he's the fence post." That's when I knew I had hit the mark.

One day while I was having lunch with a chaplain friend of mine, I expressed my feelings about those students who just couldn't cut the mustard. I told him that it was hard for me to have to drop them out of the program. I knew that dropping some students was inevitable, but it was still hard. He hesitated a moment and said "Mike, never try to teach a pig to sing. You waste your time and you annoy the pig. Just keep doing what you do. It's kind of what I do in saving souls. You can't save them all." Thank you, Father Ted.

I felt an indescribable sense of satisfaction during that tour of duty. I was helping people to succeed, challenging and molding their minds and bodies to do things that they thought they'd never be able to do, and fine-tuning leadership skills in my students and myself. What a rush!

Here is an appropriate passage by Admiral James D. Watkins, USN (Retired). It is excerpted from a book on U. S. submarines. His article specifically addresses Admiral Hyman Rickover, who is frequently called the father of the nuclear-powered navy:

> "All of Admiral Rickover's civilian and military students shared one thing in common—they all became better human beings because he taught them to strive for excellence and not settle for mediocrity. They knew because he taught them intellectual integrity, technical honesty, sound analysis, courageous decisions, dedication to American ideals, and a quest for excellence in himself and others. Admiral Rickover has said that one must learn to reach out, not to struggle for that which is just beyond, but to grasp at results which seem almost infinite. His quest for excellence in education and in the quality of people makes the difference."

Although it was over far too soon, my final tour of duty came to an end. While packing up my gear, preparing to leave, and anticipating retirement, three wonderful things happened. All of my chiefs, master divers, and instructors—led by Master Diver Bobby Cave (of the great white shark story)—walked into my office and presented me with a beautiful piece of hardwood that was laminated with resin. It was adorned with the naval officer's diving insignia, and it

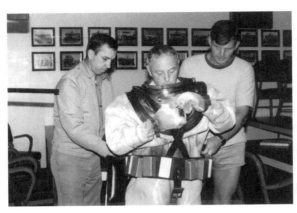

(L) Master Chief McKnight, (C) Master Diver Bobby Cave, (R) Master Diver Tom Jennings Dive School, San Diego 1989

held a brass plate with the inscription "You alone can take credit for so much improvement in just two short years." Thanks again, Bobby. It still hangs above my desk.

The next day I heard a knock on my office door. In walked a young second-class diver who previously had been trained by us. He said, "Commander, you probably don't remember me, but you gave me a second chance after I screwed up." He shook my hand and said, "I just want to tell you that recently I was in a pretty tight predicament under a ship. I managed to survive only because of your dedicated persistence when you trained me. You saved my life." My God, who could possibly ask for more?

They say good things come in threes. Next, I was called in to see my boss, the captain who was not too fond of divers in general or of me in particular. He informed me that my new detailer called him and said that I had been selected for command. He wanted to verify that I would accept the commanding officer billet at Consolidated Divers Unit at Naval Base, San Diego, for one final tour. Was he kidding? Did the sun rise in the east? He even shook my hand and said "Congratulations." I looked him square in the eye as I squeezed his hand *very hard*. "Thank you, sir." Enough said.

CHAPTER SIXTEEN

LEADERSHIP AND THE LAST HURRAH

"If your want happiness for one hour—take a nap.
If you want happiness for a day—go fishing.
If you want happiness for one month—take a vacation.
If you want happiness for one year—inherit a fortune.
If you want happiness for a lifetime—help someone."
—Chinese Proverb

THE THREE R'S

As a preface to my description of my last tour of duty, I would like to briefly address the three R's: rights, responsibilities, and rules. Freedom is a right. I have heard it said that freedom is nothing more than a chance to be better. Responsibility is a related concept. We have freedom in America, but it is incumbent on recognizing the responsibilities that go along with it. For example, a commanding officer or leader has ultimate authority. Along with ultimate authority comes ultimate responsibility. Your guidelines are your rules. Notice I said "guidelines." The idea that that rules are made to be broken is not true. Deviations from certain rules are permitted only if the rules do not directly apply to a situation that is unique and requires interpretation or deviation to meet a need. Leaders are expected to utilize the three-R's concept but adapt it to individual situations.

We all make mistakes. But excuses only exacerbate the problem or compound the mistakes. I cannot tolerate excuses. They are the breeding ground for defeat and ultimate personal and professional disaster. If you fail, blame no one but yourself. Admit your mistake and move on. How can you revel in ultimate success if you have not experienced failure from time to time? I have failed several times in my life, but I have never succumbed to defeat. When you succumb to defeat, you quit. "Quit" is a four-letter word that is synonymous with defeat.

MEDIOCRITY

Mediocrity is an offense that swallows up many people who have the potential to be successful. Imagine a workman who takes a fine piece of Brazilian walnut wood and, with an extra-fine artist's pen, measures it for a cut. After he carefully draws his line, rather than spending the time to search for the proper cutting tool, he cuts it with an ax. This workman did not expend the extra effort required to excel. Mediocrity is a cop-out.

In my younger years, I was a mediocre student. However, when I recognized the consequences of my mediocrity, I realized that tenacity was the remedy. I reinforced myself with an insatiable desire to excel, and I developed the patience and understanding to support it.

Along the way I learned that, as a leader, it was important for me to take the time to understand those who were similarly afflicted. I also recognized that in order to relate to and help other sailors overcome this malady, I needed to understand its cause. Only after the crippling disease of mediocrity had been conquered, did I have a chance to help others build their confidence.

Here is a case in point: In my last tour in the navy, I was tasked with repairing ships while they remained in the water. This approach saved the navy huge dry-docking costs. My command was responsible for all surface ships in San Diego, Alameda, and Long Beach, California, as well as those in Bremerton, Washington. All in all we had 100-plus ships at the time (1989 to 1991).

Also, our collateral duty was to clean ship hulls for the entire Pacific fleet. This was a big money saver for the taxpayers. There were no dry-dock costs, and the removal of "critters"—barnacles and sea growth—allowed ships to move faster and more efficiently through the water, which saved immense amounts of fuel.

To accomplish these tasks we had several diving workboats that pulled alongside the ships and served as mobile platforms for the divers. The workboats required people who knew how to drive and position the boats. Since the divers were occupied en route setting up dive stations, it was beneficial to have a boat coxswain (cox'n) to safely get the boat to the location, moor alongside the ship, and maneuver the craft while the divers were operating.

One morning as I was speaking with the master diver on the barge, I noticed a young sailor working in the area who was doing his best to avoid me. Since the sailor was new at the command, I hadn't had the opportunity to welcome him aboard, so I approached him. As I did, I thought he was going to jump out of his skin. I knew what he was thinking: "The captain is talking to me, a seaman recruit!" As I shook his hand and asked his name, he stared at the deck. No eye contact. Even so, I welcomed him aboard and went back to my discussion with the master diver. Following protocol and observing chain of command, I told the master diver that I would like to see the new seaman on the barge at 0800 (8 A.M.) the next day.

Promptly at 0800 the following morning the new seaman arrived. He was a young African-American sailor from rural Mississippi. I had been told that he was so far below mediocre that any effort to bring him up to average would be a waste of time. In fact, his chief had wondered out loud what could possibly have been on the recruiter's mind when he signed this kid up. He must have *really* needed to meet a quota.

I directed Seaman Smith to the cox'n flat (pilot house), and he began sweating profusely. I put my hands on his shoulders—body contact by the captain! Oh, God!—and felt him shaking. "Seaman Smith," I said, "how would you like to drive the boat?" There was death in his eyes, and he could not speak.

"Seaman Smith, you are going to be the best workboat cox'n on the waterfront in San Diego Bay. Got it? And I am personally going to teach you." (At this point I need to reassure you that when I was enlisted and serving in Vietnam and the Philippines, I was trained to run and operate dive boats on the rivers. It's like riding a bicycle—you never forget.

In fact, it's great fun to drive a twenty-ton, twin-propeller, flat-bottom, diesel-powered boat.)

I saw doubt in Smith's eyes. No, that's not right. I saw stupefied incredulity.

"Face the bow (front of the boat), hold the wheel, use you port and starboard engine controls, use your engines and rudders." Off we went.

Now, mind you, I was standing directly behind Seaman Smith with my hands on his hands. Suddenly I heard a laugh, and it was Smith who was laughing. (Laughter is a natural human response when we are surprised at our own abilities.)

After several sessions with me and other seasoned cox'ns, Smith became a one-of-a-kind. One day I heard a knock on my office door. It was Seaman Smith. He had a big smile on his face, and he was not sweating a drop. "Captain, the chief said that I could see you and ask you if you would like a ride on *my* boat!"

Absolutely! His boat handling was not just precise, it was superb. He could turn on a dime and get nine cents change, and he could put the craft in position within inches. Below mediocre? Not anymore. All it took to turn him around was patience, understanding, reinforcement, and faith. The people in his young life had never taken the time to uncover his talents and build his confidence. I spent some time doing just that, and I am a better man for it.

Last I heard, about three years after I retired, Smith was a second-class boatswain (bo'sn) mate, two pay grades below chief. I suspect that he made an outstanding chief. Way to go, Smitty.

Now, bear with me as I risk sounding philosophical. At this point in my career I started asking myself some introspective questions. Why was I fortunate enough to have had these opportunities? What luck or destiny brought me here? Why did I take such delight in helping people work their way to excellence? Why did I stick it out?

CAPTAIN'S MAST

I discovered that there were officers in my community who disliked me for various reasons. I can be obnoxious and abrasive, and I know it.

But I sensed that much of the dislike was borne of professional jealousy because I got more done with less.

One day there was a meeting in my conference room concerning a particularly difficult task. The attendees were other commanding officers whose commands would be affected by the task. We took a break. When I returned, I heard someone laugh and say sarcastically to another guy in the room, "Give it to Magic Mike, he can do anything." It happened that these two officers were full commanders and senior to me by one pay grade, but it was time. I snapped back, "That's right. Give it to Magic Mike, you mediocre bastards." I continued, "You see, there are three groups of people in this room: those who make things happen, those who watch things happen, and those who wonder what happened. I make things happen and I know damned well where you stand. So why don't you go away and "if" the problem to death. I'll be on the waterfront with my boys making things happen!" *Illegitimi non carborundum* (Don't let the bastards get you down).

Unfortunately, that outburst, while satisfying, was a classic example of a career kiss of death … sealed with my own lips. As they say, paybacks are hell. While the work progressed onward, my selection to the next rank did *not* move upward. In the remainder of my two-year tour of duty we had no accidents, performed a multitude of underwater tasks, cleaned and repaired many hulls, recovered aircraft, and deballasted submarines. Despite minor personnel problems, I had only one "captain's mast." For the reader who is not familiar with navy punishment for infractions, allow me to give you a quick oversight.

Military NJP (nonjudicial punishment) is a system that deals with minor violations of the UCMJ (Uniform Code of Military Justice). This system encompasses such violations as a short unauthorized absence, drunkenness in public, disobedience of a direct order, and the like. According to the severity of the crime or infraction, guidelines in the JAG manual (Judge Advocate General) clearly define what course of action should be taken.

The navy command level has an action called "captain's mast." The accused may be represented by a shipmate or his division officer or chief, but there are no lawyers, no juries, and no appeals. The only thing that matters is the decision of the captain. The navy is the only branch of the service that allows the decisions of the captain to be absolute, and there is a reason for that. When a ship is away from port, there must be an absolute authority. To do otherwise would invite anarchy and mutiny. This absolute command extends to shore commands as well. Because the captain is accountable for every single thing that happens aboard his command, he must also have ultimate authority. All of this harkens back to the days of "wooden ships and iron men," a time when the punishment process was held at the base of the mast (hence the term "captain's mast), but the principle is as true today as it was in 1776.

The procedure goes something like this: A sailor goofs-up and does something wrong. He is put on report and acknowledges the report. It is sent up the chain of command for review by the executive officer. If it is not handled at that level, then it is forwarded to the captain for his review and decision. My policy was to keep small goof-ups on the chief's level (extra duty and so on), but occasionally more extreme measures had to be taken. Captain's mast is about the closest thing you can get to a kangaroo court. The accused stands before the captain, face to face, and is read the charge. He is asked if he has anything to say in his defense. The CO then queries his immediate supervisors, asks the chiefs and master-at-arms for their input, and proceeds to award an appropriate punishment.

In the one captain's mast I held, the young lad got drunk and slapped around a bar girl in town. The shore patrol locked him up, and he was delivered to my command the next day. It was a pretty cut-and-dried case, but I needed to get the young man's attention. He was eighteen years old, from a small town of about 300 people in West Virginia. He joined the navy because his family was destitute; removing a mouth to feed was a net gain for his parents, particularly if he could send home a few bucks from time to time. Furthermore, since the time he was old enough to see, he had probably witnessed his old man slapping around his mother, and he probably considered that to be common, if not appropriate, behavior.

Of course, I had done a few stupid things in my younger days, but he didn't know that. For the first time in his life he had some pocket money, and he could go on liberty and rip-roar in the local bars. He was standing there staring at me, the guy who could put an awful end to his military life. With the stroke of a pen, I could throw the kid to the wolves, force him out of the navy, and possibly ruin his life. Or I could help him to succeed. I chose option two.

After a moment of silence—which felt like an eternity for this young sailor—I looked up from the lectern and asked him, "What would your mother think of you now?" He was sweating and shaking. "I'll tell you what I've decided. I'm going to put you on a suspended bust (probation) for six months, and if you don't walk the line, I will bust you down to e-nothing (a rank below seaman recruit), call your mother, and tell her what a worthless screwup you are."

By then he was shaking uncontrollably. He fell onto his knees, looked up at me sobbing, and screamed, "God, Captain, do anything to me … throw me in the brig, put me on bread and water … but *please, please* don't call my mother!" I thought the kid was going to have a heart attack.

"Master-at-Arms, get him out of my sight."

Everyone in the room was trying to contain their laughter, but the kid was so frightened, he never saw it. After the sailor was removed and the door was closed, I said, "Okay. Anyone want to take bets that he won't clean up his act?"

The master chief of the command said, "Captain, in thirty years in the navy I've never seen anything like that. Where in the hell did you ever come up with that one?"

"Well, Master Chief, as you know, we make things happen around here."

It didn't take long for that young lad to turn into a shining star. I believe he made the navy a career.

TRUST, CONFIDENCE, AND RESPONSIBILITY

Before I close this chapter, another incident bears mentioning. In view of CDU (Consolidated Divers Unit) being a relatively new command, the lack of personnel to fill required billets was always a problem, and justifying manning requirements was inherently a slow process. For example, I had a billet for a chief storekeeper, but I had no chief. The space was being filled by a second-class petty officer (two pay grades below chief).

Shortly after I assumed command, I had an audience with the young sailor. I emphasized to him that he had a great deal of responsibility and that if he screwed up any money allocations, I would probably spend the rest of my life with him in Portsmouth Naval Prison. This particular guy was extremely conscientious and had all the makings of a future chief. I had faith and confidence in his abilities.

One day he arrived at my office with a look of fear and shame on his face. "Captain, I made a mistake ... a very big mistake ... like a $200,000 mistake."

Well, 200,000 is a large enough number to get my attention. As he explained the error, I could see that in no way was it intentional. I immediately called my boss to explain. Ultimate responsibility ... no excuses ... remember? My boss listened intently and said, "Mike, you need to see the admiral on this one." Portsmouth, here I come!

After I explained the details to the admiral, he asked me what I was going to do about it. "Don't know yet, sir. I need a little time." Admirals are generally pretty savvy guys. He knew that my ship-fixing talents were a definite plus for him and that severing my head probably wouldn't solve the problem, so he said, "Okay. Get back to me."

In the meantime a huge project arrived on the table. The nuclear-powered aircraft carrier USS Enterprise had suffered a major casualty at sea. One of her four propellers was terribly damaged, and she couldn't attain the required speed to launch or recover aircraft. Magic Mike to the rescue! We removed the damaged prop and replaced it while she was at sea. An open-ocean repair of this magnitude had never been attempted in naval history. Score one for the good guys. Still, the money mistake was on my mind.

I made a decision to take the fall. There was no sense in dragging the storekeeper through the dirt. I went to the admiral's office to receive my sentencing. As I entered, he jumped up from behind his desk, patted me on the shoulder, and said, "Mike, the propeller change-out on the Enterprise was brilliant, and by the way, don't worry about the money thing. I took care of it." His words were manna from heaven. Then he said, "What are you going to do with your storekeeper?"

"I'll get back to you on that, sir." I honestly did not know the answer to that question.

I was so relieved by the admiral's response. I began to search my mind for a sensible way to handle the money situation. Then, thinking back to my postgraduate work, I remembered a story that was presented as a case study in operations management. A young, aspiring engineer approached the CEO of a company with an idea for a product that would cost the company about one million dollars and one year to create and market. The CEO thought it was a sound idea and allocated the money and time.

After a year had passed and the funds were depleted, the project failed, at which time the young engineer walked into the CEO's office with his resignation in hand. While the engineer was explaining the failure, he handed the CEO his resignation and said that he figured he'd be fired anyway and thought that submitting his resignation personally would be easier for everyone involved. The CEO took the resignation, tore it up, threw it in the trash can, and said, "Son, if I fire you, I lose one million dollars, one year, and a potentially viable asset to this company. So I'm going to retain your services, fine-tune your talent, and give you another million to make this idea work. Now get your ass out there and make it work."

The case study demonstrated trust, confidence, responsibility, and above all, common sense. The young engineer made it work in half the time with half the funds and, ultimately, increased the profit margin of the company by some $20 million dollars.

I beckoned the young storekeeper into my office and told him the story. He was a little perplexed until I explained the similarity. If I throw you out of the navy, we lose a fine sailor, $200,000, and a potential career man who can do a lot of positive things for the country in the future. So get your ass out there and make things work. He cried. After he left, so did I. Shortly thereafter I visited the admiral, told him the action I had taken and thanked him for his understanding. He shook his head, shook my hand, and bought me lunch. It was a fine lunch. By the way, years later I heard that the storekeeper made chief, senior chief, and master chief. Ah, destiny is a beautiful thing!

CHAPTER SEVENTEEN

SUMMER'S OVER

"Don't' cry because it's over, smile because it happened."
–Dr. Seuss

A fter I retired from the navy, I experienced one of the most trying and bitter times of my life. After all, I had done everything that was expected of me, and then some: the training, the billets, and the post-graduate degree. I rationalized that I had been shortchanged, and my reasoning was that many of my younger peers had been pro-moted in rank after "getting by" with mediocrity; they appeared to be "golden boys" who were punching their career tickets. Yet whenever their subordinates had a problem, their attitude was "hang 'em," not "help 'em." Their mind-set generated an element of fear in the ranks, which naturally bred discontent.

Nevertheless, in my heart I knew that my own big mouth was to blame for my non-selection to commander. My community did not cot-ton to that part of me. They alluded to "the system": "Mike, you don't know how to play *the system.* You're a goddamn dinosaur."

After pouting and feeling sorry for myself for a while, it was time for me to sit down and look at the bigger picture. Hadn't I been blessed with good fortune for the last twenty-five years? I had faced the heat of battle and proved myself not to be a coward …nor did I let my shipmates down. I lived through combat and did not receive debilitating injuries, like so many other war veterans did.

Didn't I make lifelong friends from shipmates who, to this day, call me and say, "Hey, brother, how are you doing?" We share memories and stories. We laugh and feel a well-earned contentment knowing that when we look in the mirror, we feel satisfied by our many accomplishments and contributions to the greatest navy in the world. And most of us are still here to pass on those experiences and that dogged determination to young folks who are looking for direction and guidance—free of charge.

After heart-wrenching and soul-renewing reflection, I reached a level of pride and inner satisfaction. I was ready to move on. In 1991 there wasn't much going on in the job market in San Diego, or anywhere else for that matter. It used to be that an experienced naval officer walked out of the navy one day and into a private sector job the next. Naval officers had the qualifications that big corporations wanted: experience, top-secret clearance, education, determination, discipline, and a proven and ingrained desire to excel.

However, this was not so in my case. After sending out something in the order of two hundred résumés for employment in my areas of expertise, it soon became apparent that no one needed or wanted my services. It was time to weigh my options and come up with an alternative plan. *Don't quit, can't quit.*

I came up with a strategy based on a quote by Charles F. Kettering, an American inventor: "The Wright brothers flew right through the smoke screen of impossibility." I knew that I too could succeed if I were willing to fly "through the smokescreen of impossibility." Here is what I came up with:

Step 1. The brainchild. What could I do to provide a product or service that everyone needed? What was I capable of doing that would draw professional attention? Answer? Woodwork, something I had always enjoyed. I already had a small shop stocked with the basic tools, so I started to build anything that came to mind: birdhouses, Victorian benches, step stools … whatever I thought would catch the eye of homeowners who wanted a unique item that would add distinction to their backyards. I was committed to practicality and to charging reasonable prices.

Step 2. Marketing. How could I market birdhouses and Victorian benches during a recession? Answer? I cut out little hearts and flowers and sold them for a pittance. One day I displayed my wares on the driveway of my home: birdhouses, flying pigs, benches, you name it. One lady walked up and said, "I really like those step stools, but can you make them a little smaller for my granddaughter?"

"Of course, madam," I replied. "Give me the dimensions you prefer and your address. I'll deliver them."

Strike while the iron's hot, I always say. I worked through the night and delivered the step stools the next day. My client was flabbergasted. Then she asked me if I knew someone who could assemble and install a modular closet for her. I said I could ... and I did. After I completed that task, she asked if I knew a good plumber to fix a leak in her bathroom washbasin.

"No problem." It was a simple fix. Before I knew it, I was inundated with calls not only for flying pigs and such, but to perform handyman jobs. For "marketing" I used the best and most trusted method—word of mouth. The word around town was that I was good, reliable, clean, fast, courteous, and reasonable. And of course, that I was navy trained.

When my mother was alive, I told her that if I could clear an additional $100 a week above and beyond my navy pension, I could survive ... barely. But crawling through hot attic spaces, hanging ceiling fans, and assembling barbeque grills was not my idea of a fulfilling second career.

I thought back to my childhood, when my father and I built the barn and I worked with that old, Italian stonemason, Joe Moretti. I have an Italian name, and everyone knows that Italians are the best tile and stone setters in the world. Why not capitalize on that? I was confident that I could reach back ... even thirty-five years back ... and call on my knowledge of masonry. After all, if one performs a skill enough times at *any* age, it becomes like riding a bicycle, and Dad and old Joe taught me a lot back then.

I took some time to work up a clientele, build a portfolio, and obtain a license. Then KWC Tile and Stone was born. Before I knew it, I was booked six months in advance to do some pretty impressive high-end homes. I hooked up with several tile and stone suppliers, and the word got around: "If you want quality and precision, go with KWC. Mike's your man."

Step 3. Too much work. My workdays were fast approaching eighteen hours. Between providing estimates, demolition, ordering, taking deliveries, miscellaneous logistics, and setting the product, I was working myself into a state of exhaustion. I was working holidays, weekends, and nearly every night. It was time for me to hire some help.

One of my greatest lifetime challenges has been finding reputable, trustworthy help in Southern California. I did not speak Spanish, and I needed to communicate with my employee, so cheap, illegal, Mexican labor was *not* something I considered (even though the other San Diego construction companies did not have such qualms). I needed someone who had some semblance of work ethic, would consider accepting $10 an hour, and appreciate that I was going to take the time to teach him a trade.

I tried to give a trade and career to several young men. My entire career as a naval officer was about teaching and mentoring others, but when I tried to apply those principles to my civilian business, I ran into roadblock after roadblock. Here is a cross section:

- "There are twelve inches in a foot, three feet in a yard, and nine square feet in one square yard. Where did you go to school, son?"
- "No, we don't take two hours for lunch, and we start at 7 A.M., not when you feel like it."
- "Man, this is hard work." I know.
- "You're a slave driver!"
- Excuses? In the navy we called them "My wife, she..." excuses because that's how they almost always began. "Mr. C., my wife? She needs to go to the doctor (dentist, chiropractor, palm reader, casino, whatever), and I have to take her." Or "My dog? It was hit by a car." Or "My keys? They're in my friend's truck."
- One young man suffered the unprecedented devastation of hav-

ing two mothers die within three months of each other. Seems as if he had been smoking dope and did not remember the first death.

- "Why are you always late on Mondays?"

One particular guy didn't show up to a Saturday job. I called him, and he said that he fell off his skateboard and hurt his foot. Angrily, I told him that I didn't write the book on bullshit but I had penned a chapter or two in my day. He asked if I was calling him a liar, and I assured him that was precisely my message.

"I guess that means I no longer have a job."

"You are a pathetic and unreliable worker, but you are a fine guesser."

Step 4. Time for a break. I gave all my customers and suppliers notice that I was taking a six-month sabbatical. "Going on vacation, Mike?"

"More like a busman's holiday. I'm going to build another house for my wife and me." I had built the first one back in 1984, and while it was not an easy task, it had been fulfilling.

Step 5. House built. Back to business. When I was just about ready to pull out my hair with work requests and back orders, along came Kenny (not his real name). While I was doing a major renovation on his father's house, he approached me and said that he desperately needed work and would love to learn the trade. Now, this boy stood about six feet four inches barefoot. He was twenty-four years old, had rags for clothes, and a pickup truck that looked like the Demolition Derby loser. He told me he was married, had one kid, and was destitute.

In a moment of weakness I took him on. Mind you, this was my tenth try at hiring a productive employee. I had expended a great deal of personal energy, time, and patience to cultivate these young people into viable business assets.

Here are some of the guidelines that I stressed to all my prospective employees:

Lesson 1: Achievement is 10 percent inspiration and 90 percent perspiration. When bidding a job, be on time, be clean, wear bright clothes, have a presentable vehicle, park on the street in front of the business so that your clean vehicle can be seen from their front door. My advice was simply a mixture of common sense, psychology, and good business practice. I can't tell you how many of my prospective clients remarked, "If your work is as clean as your truck, I want you for the job." Some things are just easy.

After I hired Kenny, he visited my home for more details on what to do and what not to do while working for KWC. His first comment was, "Wow! You're really lucky to have a place like this."

"Yes, Kenny," I said. "The harder I worked, the luckier I got. Nothing succeeds like the power of desire and a can-do attitude."

Lesson 2: Commit yourself to excellence; communicate with your associates (whether they are clients, suppliers, or employees); never get greedy; and have a sense of humor. If there is a problem, don't try to hide it—fix it. Don't blame someone else. Most important, use common sense. That is the glue that holds everything together. If you put all that I have told you in a blender and drink it, you will be a success.

As time progressed, so did Kenny. I found him to be very smart. He caught on quickly to almost everything. He was personable with the customers, eager to learn, and did not hesitate to spend extra hours to help me stay on schedule. Actually, as I found out later, he wanted to get away from his wife. After I met her, I understood why.

Had I finally found someone with work ethic? Throughout our association I asked him questions about his past. "You're a pretty smart guy, Kenny. Did you ever think of continuing your education?"

"Yeah, but most of my college professors were jerks."

"How about the service?"

"Nope. My brother was in the navy and said most of the sailors and officers were out to get him." (Later I found out his brother received a dishonorable discharge.)

Little "things" began to mount, and I felt as if I had to make more subtle inquires. Maybe it was just me and my inquisitive nature. I rationalized that we all struggle to find our niche in life. Some find it sooner and some later. To expedite the process with Kenny, I sort of adopted him as a son. He told me several times that I treated him more like a son than his father did, and I felt good about that. I dearly wanted to see him succeed.

Later into our relationship, other "Kenny things" began to surface … marital problems, mood swings, and the like. Again, while I was rationalizing and not wanting to see the forest for the trees, I sat him down and drew up a very detailed money and career roadmap. "Here's where you were, here's where you are, and here's where you can go. Tear up the credit cards." Kenny was $15,000 in debt and renting a ramshackle house. He never had a dime in his pocket. I should have seen the light, but I was bound and determined to see him make a go of it.

This is where I really got stupid and failed to heed Father Ted's advice, "You can't save them all." I bought Kenny a truck with the proviso that we use it for the business. He was to pay me $100 a week until the truck was paid off (no interest), and it would be his for keeps. I paid off his debt, lent him $5,000 to be repaid at no interest, bought clothes for him and his family, and built him a small shop. I also offered to send him to school to get a state license and to give him 33 percent of the net profits of KWC while he attended school and 50 percent of the net after he became licensed. Also, I offered to give him (not sell him) the business in three years, which is when I planned to retire completely.

I proposed a pretty sweet deal to Kenny, wouldn't you say? When I explained the plan to other people, they looked at me kind of funny. Of course, I asked myself after the fact, "Where was your brain on this one?"

Soon I learned that Kenny hesitated to pursue the licensing school because he had a felony on his record. He married his wife only because she was pregnant, and every failure in his life had been somebody else's fault. His wife called me every other night *screaming* that I was working him too hard. Then the bomb dropped. One day I noticed that he was especially in the dumps. His mood was grimmer than I had ever seen it. He was crying and shaking and making quite a mess of the job. I excused myself from a conversation with the homeowner and approached him. "Kenny, what's the problem?" He jumped up, pointed his finger in my chest, and screamed, "*It's your fucking attitude!*"

Kenny had never seen me angry until that day. I pinned him against the wall and told him that I had dropped bigger boys than him and would not hesitate to give it another try. He melted like a mid-July snow cone. He just *knew* I was going to break him in half. After a plea from the homeowner, I let go. I said, "Kenny, get out of my sight. Go get drunk, get laid, or something else, as long as you are out of my sight for the rest of the day. Come to my house tomorrow."

When he arrived the next day, I told him (1) that he had just killed the goose that laid the golden eggs, (2) that he was, currently is, and always would be a total failure, and (3) that the truck better be in my driveway the next morning or the boys in blue would have his sorry ass locked up by noon. I further assured him that at some time in the future … maybe not tomorrow or the next year, but sometime … I would do everything in my power to ensure that he continued to fail miserably, to the point that he would regret that he ever knew my name. Then I kicked him off my property.

Shortly thereafter, I bumped into someone who knew Kenny and knew that he was making about $50,000 a year while he worked for me. I asked, "What do you suppose he was doing with his money?" The guy laughed and said, "Mike, what do you think? Drugs!"

I have told this true story many times with embarrassment on my part. How could I have been so naive? How could I have been so stupid? There is a message in this story for all of us. If you are like me and have a soft heart (and a softer head), if you feel you need to reach all the way to the bottom to pull some undeserving soul out of the mire, look for the signs. Don't put on blinders. Kenny and those like him are the reasons why we will always have shelters and rehab centers. Beware what you wish for and always remember this: *When the horse is dead—get off!*

CHAPTER EIGHTEEN
FROM THE GREATEST TO THE X GENERATION

"When I was your age, I walked to school in year-round snow, usually
six feet or more, and it was uphill in both directions."
–Unknown member of "the greatest generation"

"Why, when I was your age, I was TWICE your age."
–Unknown baby boomer

"What's your point?"
–Unknown Gen Xer

CAN-DOERS AND RAINBOW CHASERS

A wise person once told me that she never complained about cleaning her toilet. She was just happy to have one. Unfortunately, our wonderful country has many Kennys who do not appreciate the abundant opportunities that are within their grasp. Since most of them have never really landed on hard times, they take things for granted. Everything is at their disposal ... without limitation. They don't know what it is to want or sacrifice, and they complain when something is not immediately accessible to fulfill their frivolous and selfish needs.

I have great concern for the people I refer to as "rainbow chasers." They are narcissists of the first order and have come to the unfortunate conclusion that the world owes them a living. Actually, that's incorrect; they think the world owes them prosperity. I am especially concerned that there seems to be more of these rainbow chasers in Generation X than in previous generations.

Experts say there are valid reasons for that entitlement mentality and that the biggest reason is rooted in the birth rate. You see, after the baby boom, the birth rate dropped off the table. Demographically speaking, a 1 percent decline in the birth rate is significant. It is astonishing that the birth rate in 1965 was 30 percent lower than in 1955. Why? It was a confluence of many factors: a new war that kept lots of potential dads away from home, far more women entering the workplace and delaying making a family, and the advent of the birth control pill. The generation that is now between the ages of twenty-five and forty-five has had very little competition over the years. The number of classmates in school was manageable; seats were available in their college classrooms; and they enjoyed job opportunities that baby boomers would have killed for. In addition, they have been witness to and part of the greatest technological advances in the history of man.

My parents' generation, what Tom Brokaw astutely named "the greatest generation," ushered in the widespread use of the automobile, the telephone, home refrigeration, air travel, and many other revelations. And the baby boom generation witnessed the advent of the television, early computers, and many other advances. But Generation X has seen the world transmogrified through computers and associated technology. It is easy to take the Internet and the World Wide Web for granted, but think about this: An Internet connection has brought knowledge that has been accumulating throughout the history of mankind to desktops and cellular telephones everywhere.

When I was in school, we had libraries that used the Dewey decimal system and were limited by the physical space allotted on the shelves. No such restrictions exist anymore. Can anyone doubt that by the year 2020 the ownership of a hard-copy book will be limited to collectors? Paper books will have no functional use anymore. We will have the ability to download and read any book ever published in the world for a fraction of the cost of a paperback, and the device that stores the text will be the size of a human hand or smaller.

And how did we ever conduct business or arrange meetings without a cell phone? Most of the greatest companies in existence today were founded without cell phones, but I question whether they could succeed in today's business environment without them. By the end of 2009, 90 percent of the U.S. population—men, women, and children—had active cell phones. In Germany, 130 percent. In Russia, 145 percent. Today, over 60 percent of the people *in the world* have cell phones.

With all of this marvelous technology at our fingertips, I fear that Generation X does not appreciate enough what it took to achieve all this: the sacrifices of the World Wars, the Great Depression, or the struggling economy of the 1970s, to name a few.

Truth be told, I believe that the 2009 recession was one of the best things that could have happened to Generation X, even though their parents paid the biggest price. As the economy recovers, I fear that Generation X will face competition it never counted on, namely from the baby boomers. Boomers who lost substantial chunks of their retirement nest eggs are either going to come out of retirement or not retire quite as early as they had planned. Or they may decide not to retire at all. If this happens, as it surely must, Generation X better gird its collective loins because they will be competing with the wrong group of people.

Baby boomers have always had to be *ubercompetitive* because there were always so damn many of us. We had to be extraordinarily well educated and prepared for the workplace. I'm not suggesting that Gen Xers have anything to fear in the technology sector. We'll spot them that one. But areas such as management, mentoring, selling, and marketing—these are skills we own. In the short term this process will be painful for the Gen Xers, but in the long run they will benefit greatly from the competition—just as boomers always have.

All of this brings me back to the rainbow chasers. Have you ever tried to explain to an insolent and uncaring young person what it was like to have a party line on your telephone, share one bathroom in the house, or grow and cultivate vegetables (rather than driving to the store to purchase them)? How about helping a neighbor in need … without charging a fee?

Today's economy will harshly separate the can-doers from the rainbow chasers of Generation X, just as it did for baby boomers. Growing up without competition has made a larger percentage of the Gen Xers susceptible to the rainbow-chaser mentality.

Recently when I was talking to a young person about ending sentences with prepositions, his response was, "What's a preposition?" Later when I was trying to explain conjugation to another young person, he laughed and said he had no idea what that was, but it sounded "like an incurable sexual disease." Why should Gen Xers bother with math exercises when Mr. Computer or Mr. Calculator can do it for them? I told a young man at a supplier's office that there are 144 square inches in a square foot. Then I really blew him away when I informed him there are 5,280 feet and 1,760 yards in a mile. "Man, how did you know that?" I went to school.

I know how this sounds, and I understand that the young man could have come back and asked, "But can you program or even operate this computer? Because I can tell it how big a house is, and it will tell me how many tiles you need—complete with an allowance for waste." Or "But can you explain bandwidth to me? Because I guarantee you I can find out how many square inches are in a *square mile* faster than you can enter a telephone number into your cell phone's address book." But he did not. He was, I believe, impressed. I think he learned something that day. And so did I.

I have a dear friend who has three children who span two generations, believe it or not. He is a boomer like I am. His older children are grown, married, and having children of their own, but his youngest son is only eleven. He pointed out the stark differences between the schooling and learning curve of his oldest and youngest kids, who were eighteen years apart in age. In the 1990s computer training became part of every child's education from middle school on up. Unlike his older children, his youngest child had his first computer class in kindergarten.

My friend assures me that they are still teaching the times table, English, writing, social studies, music, and how many inches are in a square foot. In addition, they are teaching how to own the *world* of digital information, a gift we boomers have come by late in life. My friend goes on to declare that nothing is more annoying than other people's kids, so he forgives my fogeyish attitude.

DECIDE TO DECIDE

I learned about decision making a long time ago. I think the best way to present my thoughts on the subject is to explain my "pier-and-boat philosophy." Imagine you have one foot on the pier and one foot on the boat, and the boat is getting underway (leaving the pier). You better make a decision quickly—whether you are staying, going, or swimming. Indecision is a decision, and it will land you in the water. The question is, can you swim?

Human nature dictates that we do not like being wet and cold. We prefer to be dry and warm. How can you stay dry, warm, comfy, and cozy and still maintain self-respect when you are forever chasing rainbows, sponging off others, depending on the luck of the draw, and succumbing to the idea of using others as a crutch to compensate for your ineptitude, lack of initiative, and compromised self esteem? Some people may think that I am overly subjective in my analysis of Generation X. Maybe so. But if just one reader experiences a wake-up call, then this was time well spent. I am not saying that today's youth must do it the way we did it. Frankly, if they did they would be left behind. Instead, I am saying that many of our young minds are not being sufficiently challenged and disciplined to think and develop in a way that is concomitant with their abilities. Your reputation is what you are in the light, but your character is what you are in the dark.

APPENDIX

PRESENT STAND

CHAPTER NINETEEN

BACK TO THE FUTURE—MY THOUGHTS

"A little rebellion now and then is a good thing."
–Thomas Jefferson

"They that can give up essential liberty to obtain a little temporary safety deserve neither liberty nor safety."
—Ben Franklin

I have heard it said that if the 4.6 billion years of the Earth's existence were considered to be a single day, the 40 thousand years of human existence would represent the last two seconds. How did we ever progress so far yet remain so screwed-up in just two seconds?

To this point in the book I have been using personal stories to teach lessons about character building, courage under fire, working through pain, personal betterment, identifying and achieving goals, and more. These are lessons we can all benefit from, no matter how old we are. Now I would like to change my focus and discuss some national issues of the day within the framework of the wisdom and logic I have gained throughout a lifetime of service, struggle, and decision making. My responses to these contemporary political, economic, and social situations are based upon my admiration for wise and strong leadership and my passion for the safety, security, and welfare of this great country.

Here is one of my basic premises: The majority of our representatives, in all phases of government, have two brain cells. One is lost and the other is out looking for it. Character and honor matter. So do knowledge, insight, and good judgment. Without these admirable qualities, we invite a whole host of avoidable dilemmas.

BAILOUTS AND CRONYISM

My dog is twenty years old. He is blind and deaf and has difficulty walking, but he's my buddy. He has given me a great deal of love and companionship over the years—as most dogs do. He has neither asked for nor wanted anything in return for the care I have given him. And even in his current condition, I am convinced that he is smarter than most government officials. Here's why: He has learned some lessons and formulated some principles over the last twenty years, and he applies those lessons and those principles to his life. He does not bite the hand that feeds him; he does not welcome anyone into our home who would do us harm; and he does not foul his own house. Politicians, as a group, are consistently guilty of all three.

Because my dog is so infirm, it is now my turn to take complete care of him, and I have no problem doing that as he has given me so much comfort, affection, and happiness over the years. He has invested loyalty and love for his old age, and now he deserves a return on his investment.

American baby boomers have worked and saved and, for the most part, invested wisely throughout their lifetimes. Justifiably, we expected a similar return. We have worked hard, made sacrifices, fought for our country's survival, helped others, and did whatever else was necessary to safeguard this beautiful land. Somehow, though, things got out of hand and wrapped around the axle. We have watched the investments we have built and marshaled over many years evaporate over a few months.

Were we at fault? No, unless we were one of the knuckleheads in Congress who voted for the Community Reinvestment Act in 1999 or one of the many lenders who threw credit guidelines out the window and lent money they had no realistic chance of getting back. When the ensuing excrement hit the blade-oscillating-air-movement device, those two groups got together again with the following consequence: Congress approved billions in bailouts for their friends and contributors—the lenders. I am not alone in condemning this despicable practice of pork-barreling cronyism, but I must rail just the same.

My wife and I will not euthanize the dog until it is absolutely, positively, without a doubt necessary. Yet Americans who have given so much have been monetarily euthanized by individuals who should be laboring the rest of their lives in chain gangs or hanged for their irresponsibility and greed. Yet somehow they are reinstated to the very positions that cost all of us billions of dollars. Rush Limbaugh said it best: "It's like putting Colonel Sanders in charge of safeguarding the chicken house."

Everywhere you turn some government official has his or her hand out. They say they need more from us, but they never admit that the shortfall they are experiencing is due to their own mismanagement of our national, state, and local "households." In the words of Ronald Reagan, "If you find a puppy on the road and feed him, he'll be at your door for more."

CRIME AND PUNISHMENT

Ben Franklin had some great ideas. Here are a few: If you steal from someone, you must work for that person until your dastardly deed is paid for … in full. If you commit murder, you will be hanged … not sent to prison. If you have fallen on hard times, the community—not the government—will ban together to help you until you are on your feet; afterward you will return the favor in some capacity.

Ben Franklin offered quite the concepts, don't you think? And what's even more impressive is this: They worked! Old Ben was the smartest, most practical, and funniest of our Founding Fathers. I'll bet if Old Ben, Jefferson, Madison, and the rest of the founders were alive today, there would be no welfare, no workers' compensation, no unions, and no overcrowded prisons. We would earn and deserve what we have. What an idea! Most likely, roadwork would be performed by chain gangs, and prisons would have no TVs or weightlifting facilities.

Convicts are sent to prison for a reason, and that reason is not rest and relaxation. How much better off would we be if prisons *really* tried to rehabilitate? I realize that there are programs for inmates to earn high school diplomas, but what if we removed the televisions and quadrupled the libraries? What if an offender were sentenced to either (1) complete the requirements for a bachelor's degree, or (2) earn his certification as a journeyman electrician? Suppose we gave an inmate the option of learning enough to become a master plumber or a registered nurse? How about if they were only able to seek parole after they demonstrated they possessed the skill, knowledge, and unquestionable desire to be contributing members of society? I'm sure the ACLU would declare that forcing a man to better himself would be cruel and unusual punishment. Yes, it would be unusual.

What about prison gangs? Here's a thought: If you are convicted of a crime and you are a professed or proven gang member, you get sent to a specific prison that houses members of that gang. Crips here. Bloods two hundred miles away. Aryan Nation? Your prison is over here. Under this plan warring factions within gangs would develop, but at least we would be dealing with folks who are killing and maiming their own, an activity that will surely lose its appeal after the attrition rate reaches 50 percent or so. Come to think of it, this plan might be a solution to prison overcrowding.

GAY RIGHTS

All for 'em. Surprised? I personally don't care if someone wants to marry his or her same-sex partner. As the old gag goes, gays should have the right to be as miserable in marriage as the rest of us sometimes are. Furthermore, married gays deserve and should enjoy all the benefits straight couples have in the workplace. What goes on in consenting adults' bedrooms is sacrosanct, but forgive the pun, do not cram it down my throat. By all means, celebrate your gayness in a gay-rights parade, but if you strip naked on a city street in broad daylight and engage in a sexual act, expect to be arrested, just as any heterosexual would be arrested who engaged in the same public display. Nonetheless, even after Californians voted *no* on gay marriage, the mayor of San Francisco stated that San Franciscans would be allowed to do whatever *he* decided, like it or not. That was the end of that.

GUN CONTROL

I am a gun enthusiast, I always have been: on the farm, in the navy, and today. The Second Amendment gives me the right to bear arms, and that right will not be impinged upon. Since laws that have been interpreted by liberal judges protect criminals instead of victims, our prisons are bursting at the seams. At this writing the State of California is releasing a large number of criminals in order to cut costs and ease prison overcrowding. The cost overruns are a direct result of providing unfathomable creature comforts to some of the most disagreeable dregs of society.

Where will most of California's bad guys go after they are released? Right back to their neighborhoods. What will they do there? They will conduct the same business they were punished for in the first place … crime. I am ready for their release, and I will repel any attempt to steal from me or harm me, my family, or my neighbors. I am the militia. Current California law says that if I am attacked by some goon (even in my own home) and I shoot him dead after he threatens me with a baseball bat, I have used excessive force. Criminals, please pay attention: I don't keep a baseball bat handy in every room of my house, but I am prepared. I have excessive force at arm's reach, and I will use it. Do not come to my house uninvited. I never used a baseball bat in Vietnam, and I don't plan on using one now. It's time for us to remember an old adage: It's better to be judiciously tried by twelve than carried by six.

FOREIGN RELATIONS

On a worldwide scale our present leaders are failing abysmally. Hatred borne of envy and religious fanaticism is directed toward us from more second-rate empires than I can name. We will *never* win these people over. I learned at a tender age that money can't buy you love. Doesn't that message similarly apply to nations? Of course, it does. Let's restrict our financial goodwill to nations who are our allies, not to those we *hope* will become our friends. Only *after* a country publicly avows its loyalty to us and shows us they are willing to back it up as ambassadors and warriors, will we write them a check.

As for our enemies, let's be clear. We must change our approach to diplomacy and change our response to attacks. In the film *The Untouchables*, Jim Malone, a Chicago cop (magnificently played by Sean Connery), said, "He pulls a knife, you pull a gun. He sends one of yours to the hospital; you send one of his to the morgue. That's the Chicago way." Well, count me among those who endorse *that* Chicago way for foreign policy. Our response after 9/11 was woefully inadequate. For some people, nothing succeeds like excess.

It has been clearly documented that dropping nuclear weapons on secondary targets in Japan brought Japanese surrender and saved millions of lives … on both sides. While they were arming women and children with sharpened bamboo spears, the fanatical Japanese were preparing to defend themselves against an invasion. But these days we do not celebrate saving lives. Instead, we hear condemnation for dropping bombs. If Germany would have developed "the bomb" before we had (and they were close), do you suppose they would have dropped their devices on Des Moines and Albuquerque? No, sir. Most certainly, we would have been counting the dead in New York City and Washington, D.C.

As leaders of the free world our approach must be to temper our might with mercy, but only for countries that deserve mercy. Our days of passing out Hershey's bars are over. Those who hate us must be made to fear and respect us *more* than they despise us. I understand this is no easy task, but our current battles will never be won with strategic retreats and negotiation. The time to discuss a peaceful end to hostilities is when your enemy is suffering from a broken jaw.

After WWI we entered into the Treaty of Versailles. It didn't work. It left Germany feeling embittered and looking for redress. Then we had the League of Nations. That didn't work either. During WWII they were powerless to stop the Axis countries. Now we have the United Nations, which doesn't work worth a damn. They don't maintain peace or security, yet we foot the bill for this organization, which is useless by all accounts. When are we going to smarten up? I suggest we tell the prima donnas in the UN that they need to pack their briefcases and go home. Then we can fumigate the building and sell it to the fine people at Marriott. At least then it would become useful square footage.

ENVIRO-TERRORISTS

I support all efforts to maintain our environment. My recycle bin always contains three times as much material as my trash can. I care about air quality, water quality, landfills, animals, and so on. But haven't things gotten a little out of hand? We depend on our present and future enemies for fuel. We don't drill or mine in the U.S.A., even when it's been proven that we could outsource and out-produce most, if not all, of the other countries in the world. Also, we have proven that offshore oil rigs attract a multitude of ocean critters seeking breeding grounds and habitats. I've seen it myself, from the surface as well as from below.

Water in Southern California is being rationed partly because of an endangered smelt fish in some lake or reservoir someplace. We are afraid to build nuclear power plants; if one sprung a leak, it would create an environmental hazard. Meanwhile, many of our navy ships are nuclear powered, including all the submarines and aircraft carriers. In addition, France fuels just about their entire country on nuclear power.

How many lives have been lost or damaged over the years in coal mines, on oil rigs, and in refineries? Thousands. Now, how many deaths and radiation-related injuries have occurred in the 103 U.S. nuclear power plants and among the 80-plus U.S. Navy nuclear-powered ships? Let me add it up for you: Let's see, now. Four, carry the one … *none!* The navy alone has accumulated over 5,400 reactor *years* without an accident.

I don't care how many times you watch *The China Syndrome* or *Silkwood*; you will never be able to prove that nuclear power is not the safest and cleanest source of power in the world. Ever since the Cold War ended, we have disarmed much of our nuclear arsenal; now we have abundant resources for powering new plants.

Environmental objections to human progress are growing increasingly strident. We should not build desalinization facilities because they might affect the ocean and the fish. Yet every ship in the navy has desalinization plants on board … and that's not just our navy. This has been going on for fifty years, and the oceans are none the less for it.

The environmentalists warn us not to build houses with lumber frames because that will deplete our precious tree resources. The truth is that there is more standing timber in North America today than there was when the Pilgrims landed. Why is that? Because of good, old American greed. The lumber and paper industries wanted to ensure that there would always be an abundant supply of this renewable resource, so for every tree they harvested, they planted two. Today these "old-growth" forests are rarely touched and never strip-harvested because we have too many perfect twenty- to thirty-year-old forests that were planted by Weyerhaeuser and Louisiana Pacific.

Environmentalists have their own internal conflicts. The wind-power people are opposed by the bird people, who fear that a fast-turning windmill blade might hit a bird. Ahem! How about putting a screen cowling over the blades?

Environmentalists are concerned that the indiscriminate discharge of methane gas by cows, pigs, and men (never women, I have learned) contributes to the deterioration of the ozone layer. Oh, please! Do these people think flatulence is a twentieth century invention? What? Mastodons never farted?

Global warming is given more daily attention and funding than cancer research. I wonder if Mr. Gore had a chance to visit Colorado or Ohio in May 2009. There was so much snow and cold then that people were dying. He probably didn't have a chance to get there because the airports were closed. And in Dallas, Texas, more snow fell in a single day in February 2010 than had ever been recorded in history.

Believe it or not, the global warming alarmists quickly aver that record cold is evidence of global warming. They simply state that any adverse weather event is the result of man's abuse of the planet. Well, here's a news flash: There have been adverse weather events on planet Earth long before there were people. What do environmentalists suppose caused the end of the last Ice Age? Wooly mammoths driving SUVs? Maybe it was the flatulence.

Ecology is a relatively new science. I took an ecology course at college in 1964. Ecosystems and ecology naturally go hand in hand. The worm feeds the bird, the bird feeds the cat, the cat feeds the coyote; the coyote feeds the mountain lion, and so on and so forth up the food chain. We plant wheat and corn, the steer or cow eats them, we milk the cow and eat fine prime ribs and porterhouse steaks. It's a system that has worked well since the dawn of time.

From time to time the natural balance is interrupted by changes that occur on Earth ... not at the glacial speed of evolution, but overnight. Along comes a volcano, an earthquake, pestilence, or a comet that upsets the environment and causes an imbalance in the food chain. At certain times in the history of this planet, catastrophic occurrences have wiped out as much as 97 percent of the species that were alive at the time.

Sharks and alligators have been around for billions of years because they are the apex predators of their environments, just as we are of ours. From personal experience I can tell you that when we enter the environment of a shark or an alligator, they are *still* the apex predators, regardless of our superior IQ. But if the alligator were more concerned about the welfare of the beaver than he was about filling his belly, he would not be an evolutionary success story ... he'd be history!

If you want to get really confused, try Web surfing in an effort to discover how many species of fauna and flora have become extinct over the years. Conservation International's Web site is an alarmist display. In one corner they solicit donations from the public. In the middle of the home page is a "countdown clock" that suggests an animal on this planet becomes extinct every twenty-one minutes, which is a rate of over 25,000 per year. However, if you visit the site of the International Union for Conservation, an organization funded by governments, foundations, member groups, and corporations (and thus not quite so prone to hysteria), they estimate that 800 plant and animal species have become extinct since the year 1500, a rate of less than one per year. How can two organizations that have similarly stated goals be so far apart? Because neither one of them has any idea what they are talking about. None of these sites do.

When I researched the Internet to find out how many species of plants and animals are alive on Earth right now, I got answers ranging from 5 million to 100 million, even though only 2 million have been identified.

Neither Conservation International nor the International Union for Conservation told me how many new species are being created each year, but I know … it's roughly the same number as the extinctions. Whether you credit God, evolution, or Mother Nature, that's the truth. If it were not true, we and all the other "late arrivals" would never have joined the sharks and alligators on this big blue orb.

The greatest interruptions to the natural ebb and flow of things are wars and pandemics … and of course, when tree-huggers spike trees in an effort to maim and kill their fellow human beings.

RULES FOR THE SAKE OF RULES

To close this chapter, I'd like to tell you a true story. Every two months or so I treat myself to a hamburger at an old-time, cowboy-atmosphere restaurant. It's not a fast-food place. It's a sit-down place where a server takes your order and you are waited on by friendly people. I have patronized this restaurant for the better part of twenty years. Aside from the fact that they serve a great burger, another reason I like to eat there is the garnish tray they place in the middle of each table. It contains fresh, raw onions slices; mustard, ketchup and mayonnaise in easy-to-use bottles (not in aggravating plastic packets); and my favorite, a container of whole jalapeño peppers. My mouth is watering just thinking about those vinegar-soaked peppers.

Recently I stopped by and noticed that the garnish trays were missing from the tables. So I asked the server why. He told me that they had to take them off the tables by direction of the Health Department. The rationale was that consumers could use their used forks to dig an onion or pepper out of the container, and that could contaminate the remaining food. "But we've been doing that for twenty years," I protested. "Have you ever had a complaint or has anyone ever gotten sick?"

"No, but the government says we won't stay in business if we don't comply."

This is government rule run riot. They've gone so far as to tell me how to eat my hamburger! This is the reality we are living in. Is rebellion not in order? Once we rebelled over the price of tea; we stormed a ship belonging to the strongest nation on Earth. I say we are within our rights … no, we are *duty bound* by our constitutions and our Constitution to overthrow a Health Department that imposes rules for the sake of rules. If we can't take back the streets, let's at least take back the food inspectors!

A reality check is long overdue.

CHAPTER TWENTY

AMERICAN PRIDE

"This will remain the land of the free only so long
as it is the home of the brave."
–Elmer Davis

Whenever I walk into a grocery or hardware store, or when I walk around my home, for that matter, I bask momentarily in the abundance with which I am blessed. It's not just the material things I am referring to but also the availability of goods and the beauty that surrounds me. I am in awe daily. One time, as an exercise, I approached a young person who was stocking the fruit and vegetable displays at the grocery store. I asked him, "Say, can you point out the apples to me?" His polite response was, "Sure, sir. What kind of apples would you like? We have Red Delicious, Granny Smith, Winesap, Gala, Fuji—anything you like." Such abundance!

Every night I go to bed and thank God for the peace and comfort my wife and I enjoy and the absence of the pain, sweat, and threat I once knew. I am blessed with quiet, serene, and secure surroundings and the peaceful anticipation of an uninterrupted sleep. Many people in this country take these things for granted. I do not. I think about the people who never had the chance to live a full life or the opportunity to savor the luxuries I enjoy, and I say a prayer of thanks for the opportunity I had to be among "all who gave some, and some who gave all." I continually ask myself, "Did I do enough?" And one nagging question remains: "Can I do more?"

As a nation we have survived tumultuous times. George Washington lost virtually every battle … but ultimately won the war. Shouldn't that be our objective today? To forge ahead and cast aside the minority that endeavors to capitalize on internal decay. Rome was the greatest nation on Earth for over 1,000 years. America has established herself as the greatest nation on Earth in about 230 years. Rome succumbed to evil politicians, sexual abominations, social decay, and an insatiable quest for entertainment and personal satisfaction. Greed was the seed that led to their demise. They cast aside their military support to fund social programs that left them broke. Does this sound familiar? And they did all that damage without high-speed computers.

President Calvin Coolidge once said, "The nation which forgets its defenders will itself be forgotten." Those who do not study the past are condemned to relive it. We are marching to the Roman drummer … about 750 years ahead of schedule. Don't misinterpret me as a gloom-and-doom guy. I am merely a realist. If it walks like a duck, quacks like a duck, and looks like a duck, chances are good it's a duck.

Are our current frustrations and exasperations any different or more difficult than in past times? No. They may be more complex, but they are not fundamentally different. We have problems that are concomitant with the times, and all things are relative. Today, as yesterday, our nation is made up of good guys and bad guys, rich and poor, the industrious and the lazy, evildoers and saints, the religious and the atheists. And here's the beauty: It takes every manner and sort of American to make America great.

If you would like to learn a new appreciation for what it means to be an American, go to your nearest federal courthouse to watch the swearing in of naturalized Americans. If it is a large group, you will see representatives of most nations on Earth. Look at their faces as they take their oaths. Gaze upon their families' faces; you will see joy, pride, and tears of thanks. And if you want to feel embarrassed, compare your knowledge of American history to the knowledge accumulated by any one of them. Their learning will put you to shame. But there is a reason for that. America is not the country they were born into; it is the country they chose.

Americans, can you visualize any other country on Earth that you would choose to live in over this one ... a country to which you would be willing to swear your allegiance while, at the same time, denounce your allegiance to the country of your birth? Of course not. It's a preposterous idea, but it's something thousands of immigrants do every year in order to become Americans.

Illegal immigration is a problem in this country, and it is a problem that we must address. But in our haste to decry, let us not forget that illegal immigrants would give all that they own to become legal residents and, ultimately, citizens of this country ... to have the opportunities that we enjoy. So while we zealously guard our borders, let us also have com-passion for those poor souls who have not been blessed to be Americans.

A TRIBUTE TO SERVICEMEN AND -WOMEN AND
VETERANS OF THE U.S. MILITARY

We lived and laughed, we fought and loved, and we smoked
and drank. We showed determination and cherished our camaraderie. Often we cried and felt abandoned after we returned
home, but we prevailed, and victory has enabled us, in our own
way, to pass on worthwhile things to our successors. Those of us
who are still around want to help others appreciate our desire
to stand by our military and their efforts to maintain diehard
American values. We made our advances and our mistakes; we
stood our duty and ate crumbs ... but we never swallowed our
pride. This one's for you:

> *We've fought the wars on many fronts at home and overseas.*
> *So stay the course, my countrymen, and help us, if you please.*
> *The road is long and like the song we've sung in years gone*
> *past. Your duty calls through hallowed halls, our purpose still*
> *steadfast.*

—Magic Mike (Cattolico)

Thank you, God, for allowing me to be an American. And while
we are thanking God, we can recall this Jay Leno quote:

> *"With hurricanes, tornados, fires out of control, mudslides,*
> *flooding, severe thunderstorms tearing up the country from*
> *one end to another, and with the threat of bird flu and terror-*
> *ist attacks, are we sure this a good time to take God out of the*
> *Pledge of Allegiance?"*

GLOSSARY OF TERMS

0800	8 A.M.
ASEAN	Association of Southeast Asian Nations
BAQ	Basic Allowance for Quarters
BAS	Basic Allowance for Subsistence
Bow	Front of boat
C/S Factor	Common Sense
C-130	Cargo Plane
CACF	Combat Area Casualty File
CCB	Combat Communications Riverboat
CDU	Consolidated Divers Unit
Charlie	Viet Cong
Chop-Chop	Eat
Chow	Mealtime
CO	Commanding Officer
Cox'n Flat	Pilothouse
Cox'n	Coxswain
C-Rats	Meals in a Box
Crawdad	Like Tiny Lobsters
Cruise	Several Months Away from Home Port
CSB	Combat Salvage Boat
Dai wi	Leader
DDC	Deck Decompression Chamber
Didi Mau	Leave
Dinky-dao	Crazy
Dong	Vietnamese Money
Duster	Medevac Helicopter
EDU	Experimental Diving Unit
EOD	Explosive Ordnance Disposal
Flag Rank	Admirals and Generals
FNG	F...ing New Guy
Handle	Nickname
Hawser	Heavy Line
HCU-1	Harbor Clearance Unit-1

Head	Bathroom
Helo	Helicopter
Hootch	Housing
ICBM	Intercontinental Ballistic Missile
IED	Improvised Explosive Device
JAG	Judge Advocate General
KIA	Killed in Action
LCDR	Lieutenant Commander
LCM	Landing Craft Mechanized
LDO	Limited Duty Officer
LST	Landing Ship Tank
LT	Lieutenant
Machete	Big Knife
MCC	Main Control Console
MK V	Mark V Deep Sea Diving Apparatus
NJP	Nonjudicial Punishment
NOSC	Naval Oceans Systems Center
NVA	North Vietnamese Army
OCS	Officer Candidate School
OIC	Officer in Charge
OPTEVFOR	Operational Test and Evaluation Force
P.I.	Philippine Islands
P-38	Can Opener
Piasters	Vietnamese Money (also Dong)
Pilothouse	Cox'n Flat
Powder	Explosives
PT	Physical Training
PTC	Personnel Transport Capsule
R and D	Research and Development
RPOC	Recruit Petty Officer Chief
S.L.J.O.	Shitty Little Jobs Officer
Sappers	Enemy Swimmers
SCATS	Self-Contained Animal Transports
Sea-Daddy	Protective "Big Brother"

Sick Bay	Medical Facility
Squibs	Small Explosive Detonators
Stern	Back of Boat
Suspended Bust	Probation
TP	Toilet Paper
TRB	Torpedo Retrieval Boat
UCMJ	Uniform Code of Military Justice
UDT	Underwater Demolition Team
USNR	U.S. Naval Reserve
VC	Viet Cong
VFW	Veterans of Foreign Wars
VNAF	Vietnam Air Force
Wire Rope	Cable
XO	Executive Officer

NOTABLE ONE-LINERS

1. You don't work, you don't eat.
2. His alcoholic breath could wrinkle a freshly starched shirt.
3. You have a choice of fifty cents a day or nothing. What will it be?
4. College was like painting over rust. You can brush it on, roll it on, or spray it on, but inevitably the rust comes through.
5. Give a monkey a banana and he could do the same thing.
6. I can cut the mustard and have plenty to spare.
7. Pain is just weakness leaving your body.
8. Solid family is an emotional basis for personal identity.
9. We are the unwilling led by the unqualified to do the unnecessary for the ungrateful.
10. Gastric courage: Close your mind, open your mouth, and eat.
11. When all else fails, improvise.
12. You can fight the enemy, but you can't fight the jungle.
13. Every day is a holiday and every meal is a feast.
14. The beer was gold and cold.
15. We ordered hepatitis sandwiches (covered with flies).
16. What came out of their mouths I would not hold in my hand.
17. There are one hundred snake species in the jungle. Ninety-nine are poisonous, and the other one swallows you whole.
18. Don't piss off the bow and drink off the stern.
19. He came tumbling down ass over tin cup.
20. Impossible is like the four-letter word "can't."
21. I never hold a grudge. As soon as I get even with the sonofabitch, I forget it. –Dee Shin
22. Providence and destiny go together like peas and carrots.
23. Adventure is worthwhile in itself. –Earhart
24. There are four ways of doing things in the navy: the easy way, the hard way, the navy way, and the Midway.
25, Paybacks are hell.
26. Never try to teach a pig to sing. You waste your time and annoy the pig.

27. Excuses are the breeding ground for defeat and ultimate personal and professional disaster.

28. How can you revel in success if you have not experienced failure?

29. Mediocrity is a cop-out. It swallows up people who have the potential to be successful.

30. When I recognized the consequences of my mediocrity, I realized that tenacity was the remedy.

31. He could turn on a dime and get nine cents change.

32. There were three groups of people in the room: those who make things happen, those who watch things happen, and those who wonder what happened.

33. Why don't you go away and "if" the problem to death? I'll be on the waterfront making things happen.

34. This harkens back to the day of wooden ships and iron men.

35. I faced the heat of battle and proved myself not to be a coward.

36. The Wright brothers flew right through the smoke screen of impossibility. – Charles F. Kettering

37. I didn't write the book on bullshit, but I have penned a chapter or two in my day.

38. Achievement is 10 percent inspiration and 90 percent perspiration.

39. If your work is as clean as your truck, I want you for the job.

40. The harder I worked, the luckier I got.

41. Nothing succeeds like the power of desire and a can-do attitude.

42. If you put all that I have told you in a blender and drink it, you will be a success.

43. He melted like a mid-July snow cone.

44. Indecision is a decision.

45. Your reputation is what you are in the light, but your character is what you are in the dark.

46. The majority of our representatives in all phases of government have two brain cells: One is lost and the other is out looking for it.

47. My dog does not bite the hand that feeds him; he does not wel-

come anyone into our home who would do us harm; and he does not foul his own house. Politicians as a group are guilty of all three.

48. Things got out of hand and wrapped around the axle.
49. It's better to be judiciously tried by twelve than carried by six.
50. For some people, nothing succeeds like excess.
51. Those who hate us must be made to fear and respect us more than they despise us.
52. The time to discuss a peaceful end to hostilities is when your enemy is suffering from a broken jaw.
53. Do these people think flatulence is a twentieth-century invention? What? Mastodons never farted?
54. There have been adverse weather events on planet Earth long before there were people.
55. What do environmentalists suppose caused the end of the last Ice Age? Wooly mammoths driving SUVs? Maybe it was flatulence.
56. If the alligator were more concerned about the welfare of the beaver than he was about filling his belly, he would not be an evolutionary success story ... he'd be history.
57. We ate crumbs but we never swallowed our pride.
58. If you find a puppy on the road and feed him, he'll be at your door for more. –Ronald Reagan
59. *Illegitimi non carborundum*: Don't let the bastards get you down.
60. Ham and eggs: The chicken is involved, the pig is committed.
61. Explosive Ordnance Disposal is a science of vague assumption based on inconclusive facts, tested by instruments of problematic accuracy, and performed by persons of doubtful reliability and questionable mentality.
62. When the horse is dead—get off!

CHAPTER QUOTES

1. There is no greater agony than bearing an untold story inside you.
   –Maya Angelou

2. If Benjamin Franklin had tried to be general and George Washington had tried to be an inventor, we would probably still be living in a British Colony without electricity.
   –Unknown

3. All glory comes from daring to begin for courage mounteth with occasion.
   –William Shakespeare

4. If one advances confidently in the direction of his dreams, and endeavors to live the life which he has imagined, he will meet with a success unexpected in common hours.
   –Henry David Thoreau

5. The problem with experience is that you generally get the test before you get the lesson.
   –Mike Cattolico

6. Nothing in life is so exhilarating as to be shot at without result.
   –Winston Churchill

7. Don't expect anything and you'll never be disappointed.
   –Eastern Indian proverb

8. Aw, jungle's okay. If you know her you can live in her real good; if you don't she'll take you down in an hour. Under.
   –Michael Herr, Dispatches, 1977

9. We have done so much for so long with so little, we can do absolutely anything forever with nothing.
   –American Serviceman's Mantra

10. You can't see the view if you don't climb the mountain.
    –Mike Cattolico

11. You can take the boy out of the navy but you can't take the navy out of the boy.
    –Anonymous

12. He is well paid that is well satisfied.
    –Shakespeare

13. Choose the job you love, and you will never have to work a day in your life.
    –Confucius

14. Every achievement was once considered impossible.
    –Unknown

15. We are what we repeatedly do. Excellence, then, is not an act but a habit.
    –Aristotle

16. If you want happiness for one hour—take a nap. If you want happiness for a day—go fishing. If you want happiness for one month—take a vacation. If you want happiness for one year—inherit a fortune. If you want happiness for a lifetime—help someone.
    –Chinese Proverb

17. Don't' cry because it's over, smile because it happened.
    –Dr. Seuss

18. When I was your age, I walked to school in year-round snow, usually six feet or more, and it was uphill in both directions."
    –Unknown member of "the greatest generation"

    Why, when I was your age, I was TWICE your age."
    –Unknown baby boomer

    What's your point?
    –Unknown Gen Xer

19. A little rebellion now and then is a good thing.
    –Thomas Jefferson

    They that can give up essential liberty to obtain a little temporary safety deserve neither liberty nor safety.
    –Ben Franklin

20. This will remain the land of the free only so long as it is the home of the brave.
    –Elmer Davis

ABOUT THE AUTHOR

Mike Cattolico, originally a native of Pennsylvania, is a graduate of the State University of New York and holds a master's degree from Central Michigan University.

He survived two tours as an enlisted man in the Delta in Vietnam where he worked as a navy combat salvage diver. In 1974 he earned his commission as a naval officer. His military awards include the Meritorious Service Medal, three Navy Commendation Medals (one with the Combat "V" Distinguishing Device), Presidential Unit Citation, Meritorious Unit Commendation, Vietnam Cross of Gallantry, Combat Action Ribbon, and several other theater and campaign awards.

Mike completed five navy diving schools, including Explosive Ordnance Disposal and Saturation Diver Training. He has served aboard salvage ships, aircraft carriers, and submarines, and has fulfilled various on-shore assignments.

Author

Mike retired in 1991 after twenty-three years of naval service; he retired again in 2007 after fourteen years in private business. He now resides in Poway, California, with his wife, Olga.

TO ORDER SIGNED COPIES, SEND YOUR REQUEST TO:

TAKE A STAND
15706 Boulder Mt. Rd.
Poway, CA 92064

Please print your return address and make check or money order payable to *Take a Stand*.

Price: $18.75 per book ($14.95 plus $3.80 for shipping). Allow five business days for delivery.